LEAD ME, HOLY SPIRIT

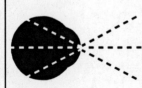

LEAD ME, HOLY SPIRIT

STORMIE OMARTIAN

CHRISTIAN LARGE PRINT
A part of Gale, Cengage Learning

GALE
CENGAGE Learning·

Detroit • New York • San Francisco • New Haven, Conn • Waterville, Maine • London

GALE
CENGAGE Learning·

Library of Congress CIP DATA on file. Cataloguing in publication data for
this book is available at Library of Congress:
ISBN-13: 978-1-59415-442-3 (softcover)
ISBN-10: 1-59415-442-2 (softcover)

Published in 2012 by arrangement with Harvest House Publishers.

Printed in the United States of America
1 2 3 4 5   16 15 14 13 12
FD212

This book is dedicated
with humble gratitude

to my Father God, for loving me;
to Jesus, His Son, for saving,
healing, and delivering me;
and to the Holy Spirit, who has filled
and led me safely and purposefully
for more than forty years.

I pray that You, Holy Spirit,
will lead me in the writing
of this book so that others
may know and love You as I do.

If you live according to the flesh
you will die; but if by the Spirit
you put to death the deeds
of the body, you will live.
For as many as are led by the
Spirit of God, these are sons of God.

ROMANS 8:13–14

CONTENTS

WHAT DOES IT MEAN TO BE LED BY THE HOLY SPIRIT?

I remember my first encounter with the Holy Spirit.

It happened during the Jesus Movement — which went from the late 1960s to the early 1970s. At the time I not only didn't know what the Jesus Movement was, I had never even heard of it. Come to find out later, I was part of it.

It was October 1970. I was living in Los Angeles and working in Hollywood as an entertainer on television, but I was suffering with the worst anxiety, fear, depression, and just about every other kind of negative emotion. I had survived an abusive childhood with my mentally ill mother, and I thought that working my way to success would silence the demons within me that sapped my strength, enthusiasm for life, and any possible peace I could have had.

It didn't work.

In less than five years everything in my

life became unbearable. The paralyzing fear, anxiety, and depression I experienced daily had taken their toll. I didn't want to live with the pain anymore. I wanted to die.

My friend Terry took me to meet her pastor, Jack Hayford, who talked to me about God. He said the way to a better life, both now and in eternity, was to have a close relationship with God. That could only happen through His Son, Jesus. If I received Him as my Savior, He would save me from the free fall I was in, and He would forgive me of all past sins and mistakes and release me from their consequences forever. I could start over with a clean slate. And equally amazing, Jesus would give me the Holy Spirit of God to live in me and change me from the inside out. It would be an inside job, but the changes would be evident on the outside as well.

Pastor Jack also said God had a purpose for my life. He would take away all my fear, anxiety, and sadness and replace them with His love, peace, and joy, and He would enable me to fulfill that purpose. I had never heard of anything so amazing before. Even though it sounded to me like a crazy thing to do at the time, something in me believed the pastor was telling the truth. So I took a leap of faith — and I have never regretted it.

That was many years ago, and to this day I remember clearly how I felt before I received the Lord. There was nothing inside of me strong enough to combat the endless emptiness and unimaginable pain I struggled with daily. I didn't feel as though I belonged to anyone or anything. It was nearing the end of the 1960s drug fest, and although I pretended to be part of it, I never felt that I fit there. I didn't feel that I fit anywhere, actually.

After I received Jesus as Lord in Pastor Jack's office that day, with Terry giving me prayer support, I started attending their church. For the first time in my life I felt a great connection there. I had been in different churches a few times before, but they always seemed dead to me, and I didn't want to get sucked into that deadness. They made me feel bad about myself, and I was already good at that. So I never went back. But in this church I sensed something remarkable the moment I walked into the sanctuary. I could not identify it at first. But I soon learned it was the presence of the Holy Spirit of God. And it was palpable.

Everyone else who went there sensed the same thing. It was impossible not to notice.

It was dynamic and life changing. It was the power of God's love, joy, and peace enveloping us, and it was touching, healing, comforting, edifying, and transforming us all. No one I knew who was serious about the Lord ever left a meeting there the same as they entered. No matter what sin, error of thinking, bad attitude, sadness, or discouragement you came in with, you left changed for the better. Regardless of what your mental state was when you arrived, by the time you left it was more focused, more sound, and more hope filled. It was the presence of God washing over you — cleansing, refreshing, strengthening, clarifying, softening, melting, molding, enlarging, and infusing you with Himself. It was powerful and unforgettable. None of us who attended that church for any period of time ever forgot it.

Nothing weird ever happened at church. There was no "What is that person doing?" because people didn't make themselves the center of attention. The Holy Spirit was unmistakably the center of it all, and people soaked up His presence like sponges. It didn't make us strange; it made us more normal. It didn't make us act crazy; it made us more sober minded. It didn't make us attract people's attention; it made us forget about ourselves and focus entirely on the Lord in praise and worship. I am not criticizing what other people experience in their churches. I am just saying that the greatest encounters I ever had with the Holy Spirit were precious and life changing, not strange or frightening.

I don't remember a time when I entered the sanctuary that I didn't weep. And I wasn't the only one who had that experience. Nearly everyone who attended a service wept at some point because of the overwhelming sense of God's presence and love. It reminds me of what it says in the Bible about when we are finally with the Lord and He will dry every tear (Revelation 21:4). In His presence we shed tears of joy, happiness, gratefulness, repentance, freedom, and relief. His love does that to us.

This was definitely a move of God.

A move of God like that is poured out for a specific time. It was already in progress when I received the Lord, and I was swept up into it in the best sense of the word. Those of us who, years later, were led by the Spirit of God to move to other towns, cities, states, and countries in order to start new churches, ministries, or lives remember it well. And we always seek to find that same outpouring of His presence again. Whenever we see one another at different places in the world, we talk about those miraculous days at the church during the Jesus Movement. And we all look for the same manifestation of the Holy Spirit wherever we are. Once you experience His powerful presence, you always long for it. You never forget.

Before the Jesus Movement happened, many of us felt that we had to be a certain type of person in order to go to church. We had to *be* good, *look* good, and *act* right. That eliminated most of us right away. That's why so many of us never went to church. We didn't fit in. And we didn't want to. But with the Jesus Movement, we felt we could go to church the way we were and be accepted, even though God was not going to leave us that way for long.

The Jesus Movement was unique in comparison with anything I have seen since. The air seemed to crackle like electricity because it was so alive in the Spirit. It was undeniable. God sparked something life changing in each of us. We felt it. We knew it. And it never left us.

I had met my husband, Michael, on a record session a couple years before I became a believer, but we didn't date then. After I came to know the Lord, we met again at this church and married about a year later. We were there for 23 years before God led us and our teenage children to another state. From then on it was always in our heart to capture that experience again — to walk into a church and sense the Holy Spirit's presence.

It is possible to walk into a church anywhere in the world and sense whether the Holy Spirit is alive and moving there, or whether there is a denial of His presence or rejection of His existence in any powerful form. Some people serve a Savior who saves, but they minimize the gift of His Holy Spirit — a gift He expressly gives to dwell in us. People crowd to a place where they feel the Holy Spirit is allowed to flow; they reject the church, and even God's Word, when they don't find either of them coming alive to them. That's because the church and the Bible can only truly come alive by the Holy Spirit breathing life into them. If the Holy Spirit is restricted by unbelief, disbelief, apathy, or a lack of receptivity, His presence will not manifest itself in power.

A church can become prideful in either its denial of the Holy Spirit or in an effusive display of Him. But when the Holy Spirit is invited to work in people — meaning He is not restrained by our fear, doubt, control, or pride — He doesn't make people weird; He makes them peace filled. They become weird when the pride of human flesh dominates instead of the humility of a repentant heart. When you are in the presence of the Holy Spirit, your eyes are drawn in awestruck reverence toward God and Jesus, His Son, and not toward yourself or other people.

I have been in churches that ignore the Holy Spirit, or treat Him as though He is a decoration they can put up and take down at will. And I have been in churches that wear Him like a badge of honor on display for all to see. I don't see the case for either extreme in the Bible. *We* don't decide what the Spirit of God does in our lives or how He manifests Himself. We *invite* Him to do what He *wants.* But we cannot let the fear that the Holy Spirit won't do what *we* want cause us to shut Him out of our lives. Nor can we force Him into a mold of our own making that causes Him to resemble *us* rather than allowing Him to mold *us* into *His* image.

This book is not about what happens in church — except that the church you attend can influence your concept of being led by the Holy Spirit. Yet you can go to a church that barely acknowledges the Holy

Spirit and still have a dynamic sense of His leading in your life if you invite Him to fill you with Himself. I know many who do.

Too many of God's people feel they can live without the Holy Spirit's influence in their life. We have a tendency to think we know best. We say, "What do *I* want to do today?" and not "What does *God* want me to do today?" Adam and Eve started that trend, and we follow along after their example. We think we can do our own thing and live without the leading of the Spirit of God, when in truth we can do nothing without His revelation, guidance, and power. We can perhaps accomplish some things on our own without acknowledging Him, but nothing great and lasting. And certainly nothing beyond our own limitations. Our lives will always be restricted without His presence and operation in them.

There should be no discrepancy between the Holy Spirit of the Scriptures — who can be seen in power throughout — and His presence in our lives today.

When I sensed the leading of the Holy Spirit to write this book, it was confirmed by two other Christian leaders who have had godly input into my life. In fact, they

21

actually mentioned it to me before I had a chance to say anything about my thoughts on it to them. That was confirmation enough for me.

At first the idea of writing a book about the Holy Spirit seemed overwhelming, because I knew that a 50-volume encyclopedia could not contain all there is to know about the Holy Spirit of God, or even come close to telling of Him and His works. But as I began writing, it was no longer overwhelming. It became clear that it was completely impossible. Yet, knowing the Bible assures me nothing is impossible with God, I have prayed fervently that God would enable me to write this book according to His will. I have sought nothing less than the leading of His Spirit every day throughout.

Because I had the title of this book right away, I knew it was to be written from this one perspective — that of the *Holy Spirit's leading* in our lives. There are countless aspects of the Holy Spirit I am not writing about because I want to focus on how He leads us — you and me — personally. My greatest desire is that you, the reader, will come to know Him better, love Him more, and grow in that knowledge and love every day. It has long been on my heart that when we follow the leading of the Holy Spirit in our lives, good things happen. And the reverse of this is also true. That is, far too many bad things happen needlessly in our lives because we did *not* follow the leading of the Lord.

When we listen to the leading of the Holy Spirit, He draws us to places of safety and blessing. When we ignore His leading — or never seek it in the first place — we put ourselves in vulnerable and dangerous positions where we can be drawn off the path God has for us and out from under His umbrella of protection. How many bad things have happened to us because we did not follow the leading of the Lord, whether because we never sought it or because we didn't heed what He had been whispering to our soul?

This doesn't mean life is perfect when we follow the leading of the Holy Spirit. We live in an imperfect world with imperfect, often misled, and sometimes evil-serving people who are not only *not* following the Holy Spirit, but they mock God, speak evil of Him, or deny His existence and persecute His people. We have a spiritual enemy who wants to destroy our lives, and he finds far too many people to do his bidding. Life is not perfect when you are led by God's

Spirit, but the good news is you will always have the ultimate victory.

When we receive Jesus, we then have the Spirit of the Creator of the universe with us at every moment, leading us through, above, and beyond all that is imperfect in our lives. This knowledge is the ultimate confidence builder. Not confidence in ourselves — for we who have not lost touch with reality are well aware of our own limitations — but confidence in God, who is *with* us by the power of His Holy Spirit *in* us. How can we not ultimately win?

Don't allow other people or dead traditions dictate your response to the Spirit of God. Forget about all of the strange, confusing, off-putting, and suspicious things you have heard concerning certain people and their experiences with the Holy Spirit, and simply read what the Bible says about Him. Let go of all fear and prejudice based on something a few of His children have said or done. Your preconceived ideas as to who the Holy Spirit is, and how He might manifest Himself in your life, will color your openness to Him. Let God speak to you from His Word. Hear what *He* is saying.

I strongly sense — and I am sure you and most serious believers do as well — that a greater move of the Holy Spirit is about to break forth such as we have not seen before in our lifetime. And we want to be ready to serve God in any way we can when that happens. In order to do that, we must hear God's voice speaking to our heart, soul, and spirit day by day through His Word, in prayer, and in our praise and worship of Him. We must be led by His Holy Spirit and not try to find our way without Him.

God wants to lead you to places you cannot get to without Him, and He does that by the power of His Spirit. He can bring you into the realm of the miraculous — not as a show, but as a demonstration of His love and compassion for the lost, hurting, or needy — and who doesn't want or need that? He can take you to the world of the invisible, which is greater and more real than the visible. He does all this by getting you to depend on Him, be led by Him, and enabled by Him. When you clearly recognize His voice speaking to your heart, your life will never be the same.

And you won't want it to be.

1
LED TO RECEIVE

God has more for you than you can imagine. But if you don't know who God is in every aspect of Him, you will not be able to receive all He has for you.

First of all, you must know that God is one God. But there are three distinct, eternal, coexistent persons in the Godhead:

God, who is the Creator of all things
Jesus, who is God's Son — and also God
The *Holy Spirit,* who is God's Spirit — and also God

God, His Son, and His Spirit are inseparable. They are always together in one another, yet separate (John 14:10–11). Three separate persons, yet one God.

God has always existed and will always exist. Father, Son, and Holy Spirit were together at creation. When He created man, God said, "Let *Us* make man in *Our* image, according to *Our* likeness" (Genesis 1:26, emphasis added). Man is created in the image of God.

God is not created. He *is*. He always has been. And He always will be.

Jesus, God's Son, is not created or made. He was *begotten* by Father God.

The Holy Spirit is not created or made either. He *proceeds from* God.

Regarding these three manifestations of our one God, we must recognize their distinctions but not separate them from one another. They are equally important. If we ignore any one of these three aspects of God, it is to our own detriment. We will never understand all that God wants us to know about Him without having full knowledge of each representation of Him. You will spend a lifetime coming to new levels of understanding about God, Jesus, and the Holy Spirit and still never exhaust all there is to learn.

My goal is not to divide God into parts in order to focus on one part more than another. There is one God, and He does not divide Himself up in order to accomplish something. But I do want you to better understand one aspect of who He is because I believe He is the least known and the most neglected in our personal lives.

Before we go any further, let's get one thing straight. Yes, God is everywhere. And He is seen in countless ways in the earth He created. But the *power* of His presence is only personally revealed to those who believe He exists and choose to have a relationship with Him on His terms. He rewards them with many things, the greatest of which is His presence.

When I hear people strive to disprove God's existence — against all evidence to the contrary — it would be laughable to me if it weren't so pathetic. For some, their unbelief has hardened their heart to the point that even if God appeared in person and they fell prostrate before Him in fear and trembling due to the unbearable magnitude of His presence, they would still reject Him.

I feel sorry for the enemies of God. I am sad they will never witness God's life-altering beauty, or experience His transforming love, or know the completeness of His presence, or understand the security, confidence, and joy to be experienced by following the leading of His Spirit in their lives. They will never be empowered to move beyond their own limitations, nor will they be moved by the magnitude and fullness of His communion with them. They will continue to be severely lacking while believing they lack nothing.

There are people who say they believe in God but not in Jesus. These people will never know the salvation, liberation, healing, and redemption He has for them in every part of their life. I have heard people say, "I could never believe in a God who sends anyone to hell," as if we get to choose the type of God we want to believe in. Can you imagine a designer God who gets a makeover into *our* image — whatever that is at the moment? What a scary thought! Besides, God doesn't *send* people to hell. That's the place they end up when they don't believe and live the way they must in order to avoid it.

It's true that there are unbelievers who are good people, who act more Christian than some Christians. And it doesn't seem fair that they will end up in hell for eternity while some horrible person, who has done evil for his entire lifetime, can receive Jesus at the end of his life and wind up in heaven with believers who have devoted their entire life to the Lord. But, again, we don't have a God we can design for our own purposes. He is God and we are not.

Others believe in God and Jesus but deny the existence and power of the Holy Spirit. Yet, without God's Spirit working in their life, they can never be shaped into the beautiful image of Christ. They will never experience Him accomplishing something in and through them that is far greater than anything they could ever do on their own. Denying the Holy Spirit will always limit what God can do in their life.

I am certain you want to know all there is to understand about following the leading of the Holy Spirit or you would not be reading this book. The first step is to make certain your relationship with God is established the way He wants it to be. Even if you have already begun a relationship with God, read on to see how it can grow deeper. There are four blessings God wants you to receive right now:

- the relationship with God you need
- the gift of His Holy Spirit you cannot live without
- the freedom and wholeness He has for you
- the inheritance He has prepared for you as His son or daughter

Led to Receive the Relationship with God You Have Always Needed

We need air to breathe, food to eat, and water to drink. God doesn't need anything. He is "all-sufficient." He doesn't need us; we need Him. But He loves us. Love is not just something God does. It is one of His attributes. An attribute of God is who God really *is*. God doesn't just *have* love, He *is* love. Because He loves us, He made it possible for us to have a relationship with Him forever.

In order to establish that relationship, there are five things God wants from you.

God wants you to know Him. He wants you to understand who He is. He wants you to walk closely with Him. And He made the way for you to do that by sending Jesus, His Son, to earth to take upon Himself all you had coming to you — which are the deserved consequences for all your sins. In exchange, Jesus gave you all He has coming to Him — the greatest of which is life with Him now and eternally with God. He said, "He who believes in Me has everlasting life" (John 6:47). He took the fall for you. He was the only one who could.

When you receive Jesus, the relationship with God you have always needed is estab-

lished, whether or not you fully recognize that He is what you've needed all along.

God wants you to receive His Holy Spirit. When you receive Jesus, He sends the Holy Spirit to live in you. Jesus said, "I will pray the Father, and He will give you another Helper, that He may abide with you forever" (John 14:16). Then God can communicate to you not only through His Word, but also through His Holy Spirit in you. God wants you to follow His Spirit every day so He can lead you where you need to go and enable you to do what He has for you to do.

Once you receive Jesus, He gives you the Holy Spirit as a gift to dwell in you in order to help you live the life God has for you.

God wants you to love Him. God loves you far more than you know. And He knows what is best for you. He says that what's best for you is to love Him above all else. He loved you enough to send Jesus to die for you so you could be spared eternal separation from Him and endless suffering as a result. Jesus demonstrated His love toward us all "in that while we were still sinners, Christ died for us" (Romans 5:8). Understanding the depth of His love for you can only inspire you to love Him more.

Jesus and the Holy Spirit are the two greatest demonstrations of God's love for you, and His best gifts to you as well.

God wants you to obey Him. He wants you to live *His* way. In fact, His laws and commandments were established for your benefit. He asks that you demonstrate your love for Him by obeying Him in every aspect of your life. Jesus said, "If you love Me, keep My commandments" (John 14:15). How much clearer can it be? Once you receive Jesus and the Holy Spirit dwells in you, you have the means by which you can obey Him in all things.

The Holy Spirit enables you to live God's way when you seek and follow His leading every day.

God wants you to give your life to Him completely. When you receive Jesus, He must become Lord of your life. If He is not, then your relationship with Him is weak. If you are more concerned with what other people think than with what God thinks, you are not sold out to God. If you only care about what *you* want and not what *God* wants, your life will never be all it can be. When you hold on to your life by trying to maintain complete control over it, you will lose it. But when you give your life to the Lord and put it under His control, you will find the life God has for you. "Every tongue should confess that Jesus Christ is Lord, to the glory of God the Father" (Philippians 2:11).

Giving God control over your life is an act of your will, but the Holy Spirit in you helps you to actually carry it out.

Think of what you long for more than anything else in your life. Trust that God will give you something even greater.

Think of the most painful thing you have ever experienced. Believe that Jesus will not only heal that hurt, but He will bring restoration to that area of your life.

Think of the greatest emptiness you've known. Understand that the Holy Spirit will not only fill that empty place, but He will also give you a sense of fulfillment in your life.

Think of everything you need right now. Praise the Father, Son, and Holy Spirit for having already provided for that need and giving you the gift that will meet it.

PRAYER POWER
Lord, help me to know You more. Enable me to fully understand my relation-

ship with You through Jesus, Your Son. Help me, Jesus, to comprehend all You accomplished for me on the cross. Thank You for Your suffering and death that have saved me from the consequences of my own wrong thoughts and actions. I am eternally grateful that after You were crucified, You rose from the dead to prove that You are who You say You are and that Your words and promises are without fail. No one else has ever done that for me. Only You.

As You knock on the door of my heart, teach me to hear Your voice and open that door, not only initially by receiving You into my life, but daily as You want me to submit my life to You. I declare that You are Lord over every aspect of my being, both now and for the rest of my days here on earth until I go to be with You forever. You are what I have longed for without even knowing it. Thank You for continuing to help me see who You really are. Thank You for forgiving me of all my sins and giving me a new beginning in my life. Thank You, Holy Spirit, for helping me to live the right way, so I can show my love for the Lord by living in obedience to His commands.

In Jesus' name I pray.

WORD POWER

Behold, I stand at the door and knock. If anyone hears My voice and opens the door, I will come in to him and dine with him, and he with Me.

REVELATION 3:20

Nor is there salvation in any other, for there is no other name under heaven given among men by which we must be saved.

ACTS 4:12

Led to Receive the Promise of God's Spirit in You

Every person who receives Jesus has the Holy Spirit in his life. Anyone who says he does not have the Holy Spirit has not received Jesus. The Bible says "no one can say that Jesus is Lord except by the Holy Spirit" (1 Corinthians 12:3). It also says, "If anyone does not have the Spirit of Christ, he is not His" (Romans 8:9). So don't think you do not have the Holy Spirit working in your life. He drew you to God in the first place. When you trusted in Jesus, you were "sealed with the Holy Spirit of promise"

(Ephesians 1:13).

When we receive Jesus, He gives us the Holy Spirit of God to dwell in us. We don't have Jesus living with us in the flesh, but we do have His Spirit living in us now.

One of my nephews received Jesus into his heart at an early age, and not long afterward he caught a stomach flu. When he kept throwing up, he said to his mom, "I think Jesus wants to get out." I love that story. His mom, of course, explained to him that this was not the case. But sometimes I wonder if too many people believe something like that, as if Jesus comes and goes according to how good they are at the moment or how He "feels" about them. But the seal of our being born-again is the Holy Spirit in us. He is the proof. It is a done deal. He doesn't ever leave.

The Holy Spirit was present and active at creation when the earth was without form "and the *Spirit of God was hovering over the face of the waters*" (Genesis 1:1–2, emphasis added). He is powerfully evident throughout the Bible clear up to very nearly the end, where "the Spirit and the bride say, 'Come!'" (Revelation 22:17).

Jesus, who was conceived by the power of the Holy Spirit (Luke 1:35), asked John the

Baptist to baptize Him in water, not because He needed to repent for His sins, since He was sinless, but because He knew the Holy Spirit would come upon Him, and *He had to have empowerment in order to move into His coming ministry.* When Jesus came up out of the water, the heavens opened up, and He saw "*the Spirit of God descending like a dove* and alighting upon Him" (Matthew 3:16, emphasis added).

If Jesus needed to be empowered by the Holy Spirit to do what He had to do, how much more do we?

Before Jesus was crucified, He said to His disciples, "It is to your advantage that I go away; for if I do not go away, the Helper will not come to you; but if I depart, I will send Him to you" (John 16:7). *The Holy Spirit was promised.* After His resurrection and before He ascended into heaven, Jesus said to them, *"You shall receive power when the Holy Spirit has come upon you"* (Acts 1:8, emphasis added). There is a direct correlation between the Holy Spirit and power.

If Jesus' disciples and followers needed an outpouring of His Spirit upon them in order to be empowered to do what God was calling them to do, how much more do we?

The Holy Spirit could not come to dwell

in people until Jesus died for us and went to the Father. That's because Jesus had to pay for our sins by His death and resurrection so we could be declared righteous. The Holy Spirit cannot dwell in an unsanctified place. But we are made pure by the righteousness of Jesus when we receive Him. Therefore, the Holy Spirit can dwell in us.

Does this mean no one had the Holy Spirit before Jesus' death and resurrection? The Holy Spirit was obviously at work throughout the Old Testament, but it was in connection with God empowering certain people to do specific things. The Holy Spirit came upon such godly spiritual leaders as Abraham, Moses, Joshua, and David, and they were led by Him. He worked in sovereign, God-ordained ways in the lives of other faithful people as well in order to carry out important things God wanted them to do or say. But the Holy Spirit was not sent to indwell all believers the way He does in believers since the time Jesus ascended into heaven.

In the Old Testament, the Spirit of God departed from those who were disobedient to Him. Saul was a good example of that. He disobeyed God, and so "the Spirit of the LORD departed from Saul, and a distressing spirit from the LORD troubled him"

(1 Samuel 16:14). But with Jesus came the Holy Spirit, who resides *in* us, who never leaves us or forsakes us.

Even though the Holy Spirit is in us and does not leave us, we are able to grieve Him and quench His work in us. We grieve Him by our sin. We quench His work in us by ignoring Him, neglecting to acknowledge His presence in us, or refusing to follow His leading. That's why we must daily respond to His presence in us and not just when we become desperate for it.

Jesus talked about the unpardonable sin against the Holy Spirit. He was responding to Pharisees who had blasphemed the Holy Spirit by saying that what Jesus did when He healed a demon-possessed, blind, and mute man was the work of the devil. Jesus saw this as a willful rejection of the obvious work of the Holy Spirit, so He said to them, "Anyone who speaks a word against the Son of Man, it will be forgiven him; but *whoever speaks against the Holy Spirit, it will not be forgiven him,* either in this age or in the age to come" (Matthew 12:32, emphasis added).

If you are ever concerned about whether you have committed the unpardonable sin — which is blasphemy against the Holy

Spirit — then you surely have not. Anyone who has received Jesus and has the Holy Spirit in them is not going to reject their Helper, Guide, Comforter, and the source of everything good in their lives. Anyone who speaks against the Holy Spirit would have to be so sold out to the devil, and his heart so hardened against God, that he is completely given over to the enemy's camp and wouldn't care whether he had blasphemed Him. Anyone who has opened his or her heart to Jesus, who has the Holy Spirit in them, would never reject Him. It would be unthinkable.

There are some who think there is no unpardonable sin. They believe that even blasphemy against the Holy Spirit is forgivable because Jesus was only talking to the Pharisees. There is a danger in explaining away the Bible this way — saying this passage was only for the Pharisees, that passage was only for the disciples, this other passage was just for the Romans — because soon the Bible is just a history book. If Jesus — who is the same yesterday, today, and forever (Hebrews 13:8) — said there is an unforgivable sin, then we must take Him at His word.

If you have received Jesus, the Holy Spirit is

working in your life. But Jesus said, "If you then, being evil, know how to give good gifts to your children, how much more will your heavenly Father give the Holy Spirit to those who ask Him!" (Luke 11:13). If we already have the Holy Spirit, why do we have to ask for Him? The reason is that there is a deeper outpouring of His Spirit that God wants you to have, and He wants you to ask Him for it.

The Bible says "be filled with the Spirit" (Ephesians 5:18). This means to *keep on being filled.* The Holy Spirit doesn't wear out, wear off, or wear down, but God wants you to seek a greater infilling of His Spirit initially, and then seek Him for a fresh filling of His Spirit whenever you want it. And you will need it because *the Holy Spirit in you is God's movement on earth.* He fills you with all that He is so you can be His hand extended. Wherever you go you take Him with you. The more you welcome Him, the more you will receive from Him, the more you will be led by Him, and the more you and the world around you will be touched by Him.

You can't live well without the Holy Spirit. You could have been a straight-A student, employee of the month for an entire year, never have robbed even one bank, and never murdered anyone, but if you don't have the Holy Spirit living in you in power because you have never invited Him to do so, then you don't have access to all God has for you. And you cannot get that on your own by being good.

The Holy Spirit–led life is the only life that makes sense. It is the only way to fulfill your highest purpose and receive all God has for you. But you cannot be *led* by the Spirit unless you are *filled* with the Spirit. When you are filled with the Holy Spirit, He becomes your Guide and Counselor. Without the Holy Spirit's guidance and counsel you will not be able to achieve the amazing and powerful life of high purpose God has for you. A Spirit-filled and Spirit-led life is a life of power.

The Holy Spirit works through you in ways that make it possible for you to do things you could not do on your own.

We cannot think of the Holy Spirit as an accessory to our life. He *is* our life. We are dependent on *Him* working through us in order to live the life He wants us to live. The reason God desires that you be led by His Spirit is because He wants to take you to places you will never arrive at without Him.

You need Jesus in order to have a deep

relationship with God. You need the Holy Spirit to become all you were created to be and do all you were called to do. It's a decision you must make to receive *all* that the Holy Spirit has for you. He is a gentleman. He will never impose Himself on you. He never violates your will. He waits to be invited to work powerfully in your life.

PRAYER POWER

Lord, I ask You for a great outpouring of Your Holy Spirit in me. Enable me "to know the love of Christ which passes knowledge" so that I "may be filled with all the fullness" of You (Ephesians 3:19). I don't ever want to take lightly the fact that You have sent Your Spirit to dwell in me, to guide and help me live the life You have for me. Teach me the deep things You want me to know from Your Word. Help me to hear the leading of Your Spirit telling me the way to walk. Give me understanding about all You want to do in and through me.

Thank You, God, that You are always with me. I long to know You better every day, so I ask for a fresh and ever-increasing flow of Your Spirit. I pray that You, Holy Spirit, will be at home in my heart. Keep me from allowing anything into it that would quench or grieve You. I don't ever want to hinder Your work in my life. I invite You to move powerfully through me, for I know that Your Spirit in me is how You touch the world around me. Keep me ever mindful of that as I go about my day and I am around other people. I want to always be sensitive to Your leading.

In Jesus' name I pray.

WORD POWER

By this we know that we abide in Him, and He in us, because He has given us of His Spirit.

1 JOHN 4:13

Repent, and let every one of you be baptized in the name of Jesus Christ for the remission of sins; and you shall receive the gift of the Holy Spirit.

ACTS 2:38

Led to Receive the Freedom and Wholeness God Has for You

Jesus said He came to give you a more abundant life (John 10:10). That doesn't mean a life of year-round, five-star, first-class vacations. It doesn't mean a six-car garage, a diamond-studded coffee table, enough clothes to never wear the same thing twice, and money to burn. It means an abundance of whatever you need in order to live the life of purpose God has for you. One of the things you need is to be a whole person. In order to do that, you must claim the freedom in Christ He has waiting for you.

The Holy Spirit will always lead you to liberation from anything that separates you from God and keeps you from becoming all He made you to be.

While Jesus forgave us of all our sins of the past when we received Him, there are still habits of thought, emotion, and action that need to be submitted to the cleansing work of His Holy Spirit. And we are still capable of sin and suffering the consequences. But God has given us a way to be free of all that. It's called being in His presence.

I want you to remember the following 16 words for the rest of your life and act accordingly. "The Lord is the Spirit; and *where the Spirit of the Lord is, there is liberty*" (2 Corinthians 3:17, emphasis added). Say those 16 words out loud as many times as you need to in order to feel that truth sink deeply into your soul and memory.

The Holy Spirit is the Spirit of liberation, and just being in His presence brings freedom.

The Bible tells us that when God was present, people were often prostrate. They could not stand before Him. The light was too bright for them to look at; His presence too powerful for them to bear. In fact, they could be consumed in His presence. Because we cannot bear God's presence either, He gives us His Holy Spirit to be with us. In the presence of the Holy Spirit we are warmed and energized in His light and fire and not burned up by it. The more time you spend in His presence, the freer you become.

Jesus is the Deliverer who came to set us free. And the Holy Spirit continues to lead us into ever-increasing freedom and liberation in Christ — that is, freedom from the enemy of our soul, from the lure of the world, and from our own dangerous and self-destructive thoughts, habits, and actions. The enemy wants to keep us in bondage, but Jesus has already set us free from his control. Jesus said, "The ruler of this world is judged" (John 16:11). He is defeated in your life now. The only way he can have any influence is by getting you to believe his lies.

Some of us experience pain and suffering because of bad things that happened to us through no fault of our own and were entirely out of our control. Jesus has total healing and restoration for all that. But some of us suffer from problems that are our own fault. And none of us can live with the guilt we carry in ourselves over the ways we have strayed from God's intention for our lives. Guilt destroys us. Our shoulders weren't built to carry it. Too often we don't *feel* that we have any guilt, but sometimes we do whether we recognize it or not. The apostle Paul said, "My conscience is clear, but that does not make me innocent" (1 Corinthians 4:4 NIV).

Paul also said, "There is therefore now no condemnation to those who are in Christ Jesus, who do not walk according to the flesh, *but according to the Spirit*" (Romans 8:1, emphasis added). When you are led by the Holy Spirit, He will guide you away from guilt and condemnation and the enemy's lies and toward confession, repentance, and a renewed heart before Him.

Often the pain in our lives comes from a lack of intimacy with God. And the only way we can experience that intimacy is to be in close communication with Him. You must be able to find a place that is quiet and private every day. Believe me, I know how hard that can be, especially in certain seasons of your life, but try. Go before the Lord and release every worry, care, person, fear, obligation, or concern from your mind into His hands. Name them specifically. As you sit in His presence, focus on His goodness and love, and welcome the comfort of His Holy Spirit in you. Let Him set you free of whatever keeps you from the abundant joy He has for you.

Ask God to help you get free of negative circumstances and negative people. Moses had to pitch his tent far outside the camp of the "stiff-neck people" in order to be able to hear from God (Exodus 33:7). You might have to do that too. If you have negative or faithless people around you who are bringing you down, do what you can to get away from them so you can talk to and hear from God.

When you are taking time to be in the Lord's presence, sometimes your pain or discomfort — physically, mentally, or emotionally — is so great that it's hard to concentrate. If that happens, bring every obstacle you can think of before Him and ask Him to take them away. *When* He does, thank Him for that. *Until* He does, thank

Him that He is your Deliverer and the Healer of your soul. Ask Him to liberate you from all your cares and bring you the peace that only He can.

Because the Holy Spirit of God is in you, it means you are never alone. You are never hopeless. You are never powerless. Because He is *in* you and *with* you wherever you go, He is never distant. His Spirit is as close as your own heartbeat. Whenever you need to have a greater sense of His presence, get quiet before Him and pray. You can get free of anything that is not God's will for your life. If you have not gotten free of whatever binds you, keep seeking His presence. It may be you haven't gotten free *yet,* but you will.

Once you are free of something, ask the Holy Spirit to help you *stay* free. Paul said, "Stand fast therefore in the liberty by which Christ has made us free, and do not be entangled again with a yoke of bondage" (Galatians 5:1). He was talking about not trying to be justified by what we do, but rather whom we know — Jesus. We have to stand fast in all that Christ has done to free us and not allow anything to take away that liberty.

God wants you to be more like Him. That's why the Holy Spirit will always be leading you toward becoming more whole. You must be filled afresh with the fullness of His Holy Spirit so He can permeate you with all that He is.

PRAYER POWER

Lord, I thank You for the abundant life You have provided. I need an abundance of all that You are. I want to receive the wholeness You have for me. Thank You for leading me toward greater freedom from everything that keeps me from becoming all You created me to be. Thank You, Holy Spirit, that You are the Spirit of liberation, and wherever You are there is liberty (2 Corinthians 3:17). Liberate me from anything *in* me or *around* me that is not Your will for my life. Set me free from every evil work. Enable me to stand strong against falling back into any kind of bondage or error again. Help me to resist being pulled into a way of life that is not up to Your standards.

Fill me afresh with Your love, peace, and power today. Make me whole from the inside out. Cleanse my heart from anything that is not of You. Burn away all darkness by the brightness of Your light in me. Thank You, Jesus, for setting me free. Thank You for filling me with Your Holy Spirit. Thank You that Your power is greater than anything I face. Speak to me, Holy Spirit, and tell me what I need to know. Give me a greater sense of Your presence. Quiet my mind, heal every negative emotion, speak to my heart, and crowd out of me the things that are not of You.

In Jesus' name I pray.

WORD POWER

We had the sentence of death in ourselves, that we should not trust in ourselves but in God who raises the dead, who delivered us from so great a death, and does deliver us; in whom we trust that He will still deliver us.

2 CORINTHIANS 1:9–10

The thief does not come except to steal, and to kill, and to destroy. I have come that they may have life, and that they may have it more abundantly.

JOHN 10:10

Led to Receive the Inheritance Laid Up for You as God's Child

Your Father God has an inheritance for you as His child that is far greater than that any earthly parent could ever provide. You and I are "heirs of God and joint heirs with Christ" (Romans 8:17). Being a joint heir with Christ means that whatever God has given to His Son, Jesus, He will give to you and me as well. As an "heir of God through Christ" (Galatians 4:7), you have an inheritance from your Father that Jesus made possible for you to receive. Your secure assurance of this inheritance is the Holy Spirit dwelling in you.

The best part of your inheritance is that you will spend eternity with the Lord. "If the Spirit of Him who raised Jesus from the dead dwells in you, He who raised Christ from the dead will also give life to your mortal bodies through His Spirit who dwells in you" (Romans 8:11). Usually someone dies in order for you to receive an inheritance. In this case, it was Jesus. And you receive this particular part of it when *you* die. Your inheritance is life eternally with Him.

But get this — you also inherit a mansion. Jesus said, "In My Father's house are many mansions; if it were not so, I would have told you. I go to prepare a place for you.

And if I go and prepare a place for you, *I will come again and receive you to Myself; that where I am, there you may be also*" (John 14:2–3, emphasis added). Jesus has prepared this mansion for you for all eternity when you leave this earth to be with Him. You can trust that this great inheritance is there for you. Praise God, anyone?

However, your inheritance from your Father God is not just in the next life, as if that wouldn't really be enough to look forward to. It is in this life too. You have already received a great part of your inheritance with the indwelling presence of His Holy Spirit. In fact, He is your guarantee that you will be in heaven one day. The Holy Spirit is God's hand extended from heaven to you. And when it is time for you to go there, the Holy Spirit will make sure you arrive home in a timely manner. Just as He leads you here on earth, He will lead you into eternity.

God says the hairs on your head are all numbered and you are more valuable than many sparrows (Matthew 10:29–31). It's safe to assume that God cares about every aspect of your life. And part of your inheritance is His provision, protection, deliverance, enablement, and so much more. (More of that in the chapters to come.) You have a destiny. The word "predestined" means that there is an appointed destiny for anyone who receives Jesus. You are destined for great things. The Holy Spirit *in* you is the guarantee of that inheritance too.

Part of receiving an inheritance is that you have to know it's there in order to receive it. You can be sent letters about it (the Bible), but if you don't open them up and read them, you won't know what it is you have inherited. And you won't know what to do to possess it.

There is a lock on one of my suitcases that is difficult to unlock. First I have to dial in the right combination, but then I have to pull down on the latch extremely hard in order to open it. When I wasn't sure I had the right combination, I didn't pull it hard enough because I was afraid I would break the lock. But once I knew for certain I had the correct combination, I felt emboldened to pull on the latch as hard as I could, knowing the lock would open. But I would never have pulled on it that hard if I didn't know for sure I had the right combination.

There is a window in our house that is also hard to open. I have to turn the handle very hard in order to open it. If I wasn't sure it would open, I would never turn the handle with that much force. When we first moved into the house, I assumed the window latch was broken. But that's because I didn't turn it hard enough. So for months I never opened the window. One day someone showed me how hard I needed to turn it in order to open it, and I never had a problem with it again. I could have been enjoying fresh air all those months, but because I didn't know the truth, I never opened the window.

My point is that too often, because we don't understand the truth in our lives, we don't give enough effort toward opening up and possessing what is there for us. We aren't sure we have the right combination or enough strength to open the latch. We just have to know the truth about what is possible for us and what to do to make it happen in our lives. When you know what the truth is, and you know what the promise is, and you understand what your inheritance is, you can press in harder than you might normally do in order to receive what has already been provided for you.

God told His people that if they kept His commandments, and loved Him, and walked in all His ways, holding fast to Him, then He would drive out all who opposed them and kept them from receiving all He had for them (Deuteronomy 11:22–23). He said, "Every place on which the sole of your foot treads shall be yours" (Deuteronomy 11:24). That means they would possess all that God promised. The same is true for you today. If you love and obey God, and follow the leading of His Spirit, you can posses the inheritance promised to you as God's child.

PRAYER POWER

Lord, I come before You and thank You for the inheritance You have given me as a child of Yours. Deepen my understanding of what Jesus accomplished on the cross. Speak to me about the inheritance I have because of what Jesus has done. Thank You that I am a joint heir with Christ. Help me to understand all You have given me and how to possess it in my life. Show me all I need to unlock and see in Your Word. Reveal things I have not seen before and bring them alive in me in ways I have not seen. Holy Spirit, teach me what You want me to see. I come before You now and ask You to speak to my heart about whatever You want me to hear.

Thank You, God, that You are my

heavenly Father and You have made it possible for me to be called Your child (1 John 3:1). Enable me to see what it means to be Your child and inherit all You have for me. Thank You, Jesus, for the mansion You have prepared for me in heaven. Thank You that Your promises are true and You always keep them perfectly. Reveal Yourself to me in ever-deepening ways. I seek to know You more each day. Help me to open up to all You have provided for my life.

In Jesus' name I pray.

WORD POWER

Whatever you do, do it heartily, as to the Lord and not to men, knowing that from the Lord you will receive the reward of the inheritance; for you serve the Lord Christ.

COLOSSIANS 3:23–24

The Spirit Himself bears witness with our spirit that we are children of God, and if children, then heirs — heirs of God and joint heirs with Christ, if indeed we suffer with Him, that we may also be glorified together.

ROMANS 8:16–17

2
LED TO BE FILLED

One of the worst nightmares I have ever had since I became a believer was when I'd only been a Christian for a few years. I dreamed I had given in to sin and lost the infilling of the Holy Spirit and His anointing on me. I had terrible remorse and felt devastated by it. When I woke up, I knew from Scripture that this could never really happen because God forgives us of all sin when we repent and confess it. But I believe that this dream had to do with my calling and future ministry. It was a warning that temptations would come and I was not to give in to them, not even in my mind. The thought of losing the Holy Spirit is horrifying. But so is the thought of people not opening up to everything He has for them. And that *can* happen.

You must not see Jesus as your Savior only and nothing else — even though that would be more than enough. You must also see

Him as the One who empowers you to live the life God has for you. The way He does that is by giving you His Holy Spirit to spring up in you like a well that never runs dry. Only this water is spiritual and eternal and is continuously fresh and flowing, and it brings you everything you need for life.

Jesus referred to the Holy Spirit as living water. When He first asked the woman at the well for a drink of water, He said, "Whoever drinks of this *water* will thirst again, but *whoever drinks of the water that I shall give him will never thirst.* But the water that I shall give him will *become* in him *a fountain of water springing up into everlasting life*" (John 4:13–14, emphasis added).

The Holy Spirit is the fountain Jesus spoke of that springs up in us for the rest of our life on earth.

Later, Jesus spoke again about a *continuous flow of rivers from our heart* that comes from the Holy Spirit. He said, " 'He who believes in Me, as the Scripture has said, *out of his heart will flow rivers of living water.'* But this He spoke concerning the Spirit, whom those believing in Him would receive; for *the Holy Spirit was not yet given,* because Jesus was not yet glorified" (John 7:38–39, emphasis added). These rivers of living water come from an eternal spring — the

Holy Spirit — and are a constant source and endless supply of all God is.

The first outpouring of the Holy Spirit after Jesus' resurrection happened at Pentecost when His disciples were waiting where He had told them to. "Suddenly there came a sound from heaven, as of a rushing mighty wind, and it filled the whole house where they were sitting" (Acts 2:2). This initial manifestation of the Holy Spirit's presence coming to dwell in them must have been wondrous — the most amazing, life-changing experience. But in case you are worried, that is not the way it happens now, although I don't doubt that it could. If you have received Jesus, you have the Holy Spirit in you. But there is an even greater outpouring of His Spirit that He wants you to open up to as He fills you with all that He is.

This means there is a flow of this same living water Jesus spoke of for you. It does not run out. You will never thirst again if you have it. But you won't receive the full flow of this living water if you never thirst for it, either. Every time you seek a fresh flow of His Spirit in you, the rivers of living water are released.

The Holy Spirit is God *with* us. He is the means by which God shares Himself with us. We don't earn His presence; we *seek* His presence. We don't have to beg for His presence; He waits for us to *choose* His presence. The Holy Spirit is a gift from the Lord. And we need to open up and receive all He has given us.

If you were to prepare the most wonderful gift you could think of for someone you love, and then when you offered it to that person they refused to take it, you would feel hurt and rejected. It would be a slap in your face. You would think that the recipient did not love you enough to consider whether the gift was something that was especially chosen for them by you.

The reasons people do that are varied. It could be because they don't want to be obligated to give you anything in return. Or they don't feel worthy to receive anything. Or they can't give you anything of that same value. Or they're afraid you want something in return from them that they don't want to give. Or they don't like you and want you to know it. Whatever the reason, it hurts you, the giver. It makes you feel that your gift is not good enough or that you are not valued enough in their eyes.

The same is true when we reject the gift of God's Spirit. It shows that we don't respect God enough to believe His Word.

Or we have made up our own minds about what we will receive from Him and what we won't. When we don't receive all that the Holy Spirit has to offer us, we reject the gift Jesus paid the price for us to have.

God fills you with Himself in order to help you become more than you are able to be on your own.

There is so much to understand about the Holy Spirit, but as you open up to Him, He will teach you about Himself. He has countless gifts He wants you to receive, such as His power and might, truth and understanding, wisdom and revelation, and love and hope, to name just a few.

Led to Be Filled with His Power and Might

When we have the indwelling Holy Spirit, we have the source of God's power within us. As believers in Jesus, the Holy Spirit gives us access to the same amazing power that raised Jesus from the dead. And just as He raised Jesus up at the end of His life on earth, that same power will raise you up at the end of your life as well. There is no greater power than that.

God can do far more in your life than you ever dreamed possible because of the power of His Spirit working in you.

The power of the Holy Spirit in us is

described as *dunamis* in the Greek language. Our word "dynamite" comes from it. Paul said, "Our gospel did not come to you in word only, but also in power, and in the Holy Spirit" (1 Thessalonians 1:5). That means an explosion of power.

You don't want to live "having a form of godliness, but denying its power" (2 Timothy 3:5). You want a dynamic life of Spirit-ignited power.

God doesn't want you to merely acknowledge His existence. He doesn't want an uninspired relationship with you; He wants it to be explosive! He wants you to look forward to being with Him every day and trusting Him for everything you need. You should not have a half-life where you say, "I'm kind of born-again. I sort of received Jesus, and I have a little bit of the Holy Spirit in me sometimes." Either you are born-again or you are not, and you are filled with the Holy Spirit or you are not. He doesn't half fill, barely fill, or sort of fill. He fills. Don't let Him be watered down in your life.

The Holy Spirit is always moving, and He keeps on filling you. You know how life can sometimes feel as though you are standing still? If you are led by the Holy Spirit, you are always going forward. Like a river. Like a deep water well. If you are standing still, you are actually going backward.

The Holy Spirit has the power to change your life, and that starts with refining you. John the Baptist was speaking about Jesus when he said, "He will baptize you with the Holy Spirit and fire" (Matthew 3:11). He is not talking about a real fire in *this* realm. It *is* a real fire, but it's in the spirit realm. You won't be burned by it, but it is a consuming fire in that the Holy Spirit will burn up — as in "refine" — all the dross in us that is not supposed to be there. He will refine us like gold by filling us with more of Himself and burning away everything that is not of Him.

The Holy Spirit gives you the strength you need in order to live the life He has for you. Without the Holy Spirit giving us His strength, we are unable to face what is ahead. We cannot overcome our tendency toward sin. We don't have courage to face our enemy. Without the Holy Spirit giving us strength, we can become like "children, tossed to and fro and carried about with every wind of doctrine, by the trickery of men" (Ephesians 4:14). Paul prayed for the Ephesian believers "to be *strengthened with*

might through His Spirit in the inner man"
(Ephesians 3:16, emphasis added). We need
that as well.

It is not a sign of weakness to depend on
God, because our weakness means His
strength will be evident. When Paul asked
God to remove an affliction he had, God
said, "My grace is sufficient for you, for My
strength is made perfect in weakness." In
response to that Paul said, "I will rather
boast in my infirmities, that the power of
Christ may rest upon me . . . *For when I am
weak, then I am strong*" (2 Corinthians
12:9–10, emphasis added). We must acknowledge our own weaknesses and recognize that God is the only source of our
strength.

That's powerful!

In the Old Testament, whenever Samson
needed supernatural strength, *"the Spirit of
the LORD came mightily upon him"* to enable
him to do what he needed to do (Judges
14:6, emphasis added). In one instance he
tore a lion apart with his bare hands. In
another he killed thirty men (Judges 14:19).
He used the jawbone of a donkey to kill a
thousand Philistine men who were Israel's
enemy (Judges 15:15). And God empowered him to become a judge over Israel for
20 years.

Samson knew he had been consecrated to the Lord, and he was not to cut his hair or he would lose his supernatural strength. Nevertheless, he did not obey God. He became involved with Delilah, and his lust for her became more important than his love of God. An immoral lifestyle always takes away our God-given wisdom. He foolishly told her the secret of his strength, saying, "If I am shaven, then my strength will leave me, and I shall become weak, and be like any other man" (Judges 16:17). Samson knew he was empowered by the Holy Spirit of God, yet he didn't treasure that gift. He took it for granted and squandered it.

As he was asleep on Delilah's lap, the Philistines cut off his hair. When he woke up, he didn't even realize he had lost all his strength because *the Spirit of the Lord had departed from him.* The Philistines put out his eyes and imprisoned him. While he was in prison, his hair grew back and God allowed his strength to return one more time, so Samson had a last chance to do God's will. When the Philistine people brought him into their arena for sport, he pulled down the supporting pillars of the temple where the Philistines had gathered, and he killed more in death — including himself —

than he had in his lifetime.

The Holy Spirit gives *you* the power and strength you need in order to do what He calls you to do. But it must never be misused for selfish gain. Only for God's will.

The Holy Spirit is the power of God flowing through you, and that puts you on solid ground, like a house built on rock. The house I live in now is built on solid rock. I know this because we had to dynamite a hole in the ground big enough to build our basement, and I heard about it from all the neighbors. They said the entire neighborhood shook. I felt bad about that for them, but I felt good about the house. When I am in the house, I can always feel its solidness. We have lived in other houses that were not built on a rock, and they felt different — as if they could blow away in a storm or come down in an earthquake. In fact, one of them did. It was destroyed in an earthquake. Fortunately, we were led by the Holy Spirit to move out of it before we sold it, and we were not in the house when the earthquake happened. I clearly heard the Spirit speak to me that we were to leave our house in Los Angeles, even though I loved everything about it, and move to Tennessee. That's how we escaped the Northridge earthquake of

1994 — by following the leading of the Holy Spirit.

When we build our spiritual house on the solid rock of Jesus' work on the cross, we are filled with the steadfast power of the Holy Spirit and nothing can shake or destroy us.

The Holy Spirit gives you access to all that God is — including His power — but you don't control that access. The Holy Spirit empowers us according to His will. *He* guides *us. We* don't guide *Him* or tell Him what to do. "Who has directed the Spirit of the LORD?" (Isaiah 40:13).

God is omnipotent. This means He is all-powerful. It is not *our* power that accomplishes anything. " 'Not by might nor by power, but by My Spirit,' says the LORD of hosts" (Zechariah 4:6). He empowers those who serve Him, as He sees fit, in order to do His will. His power is not for our own personal use, even though His power benefits us personally.

I have seen people try to force the Holy Spirit to do what they want Him to do. They want Him to heal now, manifest now, and empower now. But they don't want to come humbly *before* Him, seeking Him, inviting Him, and surrendering to Him. We cannot be like the magician in the Bible who tried to buy the Holy Spirit's power from Jesus' disciples. Peter said to him, "Your money perish with you, because you thought that the gift of God could be purchased with money!" (Acts 8:20). The power of the Holy Spirit cannot be bought, demanded, or used for selfish motives. We must always weigh our reasons for desiring His power to work through us. The key is to stay close to God and remain humble before Him.

The Holy Spirit empowers us to do what He has for us to do. The power of the Holy Spirit is all *His.* We have nothing to do with generating the power, but we must *co-operate* with Him in order to see His power work *in* and *through* us. When we cooperate with the Holy Spirit, things happen in our lives that will not happen if we don't. God wants us to live *His* way by obeying His laws and commandments and following where His Spirit leads us. When we work with Him by obeying Him, inviting Him, welcoming Him, and worshipping Him — Father, Son, and Holy Spirit — He gives us what we need in order to do what He has called us to do. Whatever God gives us to do is accomplished only by the power of His Holy Spirit working in us.

God wants you to understand the working

of His Spirit in your life. He knows what is best for you, and that's why He wants you to acknowledge Him, desire to know Him better, long to hear Him, and learn to follow Him. But you cannot do all this without the power of His Holy Spirit manifesting Himself in your life. You must desire it in order to serve God and do His will.

PRAYER POWER

Lord, I thank You for the gift of Your Holy Spirit in me. Help me to never restrict the Spirit's flow moving in and through me, changing me into Your likeness and touching others for Your kingdom. I pray for a fresh filling of Your Spirit right now — greater than I have known before. Thank You, Holy Spirit, for Your power and might on my behalf. Thank You that You give me access to Your power for Your purposes. I know that it is not by my strength or power, but by the power of Your Spirit that I can do great things for You (Zechariah 4:6).

Thank You that rivers of Your living water flowing in me will keep me from ever thirsting again. Thank You for Your dynamite-level power that can change the course of anything in my life that is headed in the wrong direction. Thank You that Your Spirit in me is "a fountain of water springing up into everlasting life" (John 4:14) and is a source of power beyond anything I can imagine. I don't ever want to even attempt to misuse Your power in any selfish way for my own personal gain. Keep my heart pure before You at all times. Help me to be a vessel through which Your power can manifest itself to serve Your purposes. In Jesus' name I pray.

WORD POWER

Be strong in the Lord and in the power of His might.

EPHESIANS 6:10

The message of the cross is foolishness to those who are perishing, but to us who are being saved it is the power of God.

1 CORINTHIANS 1:18

Led to Be Filled with His Truth and Understanding

The Holy Spirit is referred to as the Spirit of truth. Jesus said, "When He, the Spirit of truth, has come, He will guide you into all truth" (John 16:13). The Spirit of truth will help you to know the truth. He will speak a word from God to your heart and give you a sense of what is true about everything.

The Holy Spirit enables us to discern the truth from a lie. There are spirits of deception everywhere in our world today. A lying spirit is even welcomed in some circles. The people in these groups believe it's good to lie in order to get what they want. We, on the other hand, believe in the truth — God's truth — and we live by it.

The Holy Spirit gives you great understanding of what is true and what is false. He helps you to know in your spirit when someone is lying to you and when they are telling the truth. When you follow the leading of the Holy Spirit, you will gain an understanding of what is true and what isn't that you didn't have before.

The Holy Spirit can give you knowledge of a matter. Your heart and mind can be illuminated in a way they could not be without the His enlightenment. When you receive that kind of understanding, it is not an uncertain thing. You *know* it is from God. We don't want to be "always learning and never able to come to the knowledge of the truth" (2 Timothy 3:7). We want to *know* the truth, and the Spirit of truth will tell us that.

Ahab, king of Israel, asked Jehoshaphat, king of Judah, to join him and go to war against their common enemy (2 Chronicles 18:2). But King Jehoshaphat told King Ahab *he should inquire of the Lord first.* So King Ahab gathered four hundred prophets who said that the two kings should go to war and God would deliver the enemy into their hands (2 Chronicles 18:4–5).

King Jehoshaphat, on the other hand called for Micaiah, the prophet of the Lord, to come and give them his word from God about this. Micaiah said, "Whatever my God says, that I will speak" (2 Chronicles 18:13). He lived by the truth of God and would never violate that. Micaiah told King Jehoshaphat that God had sent *a lying spirit to be in the mouth of Ahab's prophets* so that they would persuade Ahab to go to war and be struck down (2 Chronicles 18:19–22). This happened so God could bring judgment upon Ahab for his sins.

King Ahab and King Jehoshaphat both ignored Micaiah — the only prophet speaking the truth from God — and believed the four hundred prophets who were guided by a lying spirit. As a result, King Ahab was killed in battle, even though he disguised himself to hide his identity. King Jehoshaphat was *not* killed because *he cried out to God* when he saw what was happening, and God helped him to escape (2 Chronicles 18:31).

This story illustrates how we must seek the truth from God and not try to find someone to justify what *we want* to do. And even if we have believed a lie and have acted on it, when we turn to God with our whole heart, He is merciful to forgive us and protect us from our own error. This is why we must always pray that the counselors we have are aligned with the Spirit of truth.

When you live *in* the truth and *by* the truth, the Holy Spirit of truth in you will guide you in all truth. You will have a sense of what is true and what is not. This is extremely important in these days where deception is rampant. Without that sense of what is true you can be deceived and make terrible mistakes in your decisions. You can trust someone you shouldn't. You can do something you think is right and find out it was the wrong thing to do.

One time my husband hired a man to do some work on the outside of our house. The man wanted half the money in advance. It was a sizable sum. My husband told me to write the check to him, but I sensed the worker was not telling us the truth. My husband insisted and I did what he wanted without telling him clearly how I was feeling about it. The man took the money and never came back. I vowed then to never again go against what the Holy Spirit was telling me about the honesty of someone.

There are times when you can almost see the lie on someone's face when they are speaking it to you because it is revealed to you by the Holy Spirit of truth.

You cannot afford to make decisions for your life based on a lie. You must be able to discern a lie from the truth. The lying habit that has overtaken so many people is no doubt something you will be faced with if you haven't already. There will be a decision you must make, a crossroads where you need to decide which way to go, a person you have to know if you can trust, a situation in which you cannot afford to misread what has happened, a paper you have to sign and you need to determine whether everything you were told about it is correct — and you absolutely must hear the still small voice of the Spirit of truth showing you what the truth is and what it is not. Ask Him to lead you in all truth and give you understanding. It could be the difference between life and death someday.

PRAYER POWER

Lord, thank You that I have the mind of Christ, and because of that I can know things I need to understand. Thank You, Holy Spirit of truth, that You have filled me with Your truth and understanding. I know I cannot begin to see the truth without Your Spirit filling me with that knowledge. Keep me undeceived. Help me to never be influenced by a lying spirit — even in the mouth of someone who is supposed to be Your messenger. I want to be influenced only by people in my life who I know are determined to hear from only You. Keep me from being misled. Enable me to hear Your voice above all others so that I can always distinguish the truth from a lie.

Lord, give me the ability to understand Your counsel to me. Instruct me by the power of Your Spirit of counsel within me. Give me counsel about everything I do and every decision I make. Thank You that "You will guide me with Your counsel, and afterward receive me to glory" (Psalm 73:24). Give me the truth, knowledge, and understanding I need in order to make right choices and decisions about every person and every situation. Lead me always in the way of truth.

In Jesus' name I pray.

WORD POWER

We have received, not the spirit of the world, but the Spirit who is from God, that we might know the things that have been freely given to us by God.

1 CORINTHIANS 2:12

When the Helper comes, whom I shall send to you from the Father, the Spirit of truth who proceeds from the Father, He will testify of Me.

JOHN 15:26

Led to Be Filled with His Wisdom and Revelation

Have you ever noticed that people who do not have godly wisdom have no common sense? They discern nothing. They may have book knowledge, but no wisdom about it. That's why they do such stupid things. When we don't have godly wisdom, we do stupid things too. The Holy Spirit of God in

79

us gives us the wisdom and revelation we need.

When you hear of people in the news who throw their lives away for the dumbest reasons, it is because they do not have any wisdom from God. They are either godless, or they have a designer god who is made in their image and theoretically does what they want him to do. They don't know the all-wise God of the universe; therefore, they are not connected to Him through His Spirit of wisdom and revelation living in them. True wisdom and revelation come only from God by the power of His Spirit. And godly wisdom produces good common sense.

Having the Holy Spirit in you allows you to know certain things you would otherwise not know. For example, have you ever sensed something disturbing about a person and it turned out to be completely accurate, yet you had nothing to base it on outside of some inner knowledge? That is the leading of the Holy Spirit. God will reveal things to you about a person's character. You may not be able to prove it right then, but you can act on that knowledge because of it.

Have you ever prayed to know what life-altering decision to make, and at some point you just knew what to do? That is the leading of the Spirit. We can never become self-assured about that because this doesn't mean we know everything. It means we can know the things God wants us to know.

The Holy Spirit will give us wisdom and revelation about something when we ask Him for it.

It was prophesied of Jesus that "the Spirit of wisdom and understanding" would rest upon Him (Isaiah 11:2). That same Spirit in Him lives in you. That's why you can be wise and not foolish when you are led by the Holy Spirit to make choices.

Paul told the Ephesians that he prayed that "the God of our Lord Jesus Christ, the Father of glory" would "*give to you the spirit of wisdom and revelation* in the knowledge of Him" (Ephesians 1:17, emphasis added). He prayed this so their eyes would be opened to the truth. Paul didn't just talk to people *about* Jesus. He had an encounter *with* Jesus. And Jesus gave Paul the revelation he needed in order to do what God called him to do. He knew what he was talking about.

Wisdom and revelation are two things we cannot live without. Having godly wisdom helps you to know the practical things to do to make your life work. Having revelation from God gives you insight that you would not have otherwise. Revelation is when God opens your eyes to see what you need to see.

Revelation gives you insight into God's Word. And God reveals things about Himself as well. The kingdom of God is a mystery and cannot be understood without revelation from God. God says, "Call to Me, and I will answer you, and show you great and mighty things, which you do not know" (Jeremiah 33:3). You can take Him at His Word.

There is an obvious connection between walking with the leading of the Holy Spirit and having the wisdom of God.

There are many stories in the Bible of people who lacked godly wisdom and did stupid and terrible things. King Saul is a great example. He was afraid of David because he saw that *"David behaved wisely in all his ways, and the LORD was with him"* (1 Samuel 18:14, emphasis added). Saul recognized that David followed God closely and he did not — that God was with David and not with him. Saul saw that God loved David and so did his daughter Michal and his son Jonathan (1 Samuel 18:1,28). David even became "highly esteemed" among the people, while Saul's reputation diminished in their eyes (1 Samuel 18:30). All this frightened Saul and added to his jealousy and determination to destroy David.

Without any godly wisdom — because he didn't even try to seek the leading of the Holy Spirit — Saul continued to sink into greater sin by planning to murder David. Without the presence of the Holy Spirit, and having no desire for His leading — and as a result no godly wisdom — Saul became insanely jealous of David and threatened by him, even though David had done no harm. When Jonathan, Saul's son, came to David's defense, Saul even tried to kill his own son.

We know the story of how God appeared to Solomon — David's son who became king after David — in a dream. God asked Solomon what he wanted, and Solomon humbly asked for wisdom and knowledge. God was so pleased with what Solomon asked for that He said, "Because this was in your heart, and you have not asked riches or wealth or honor or the life of your enemies, nor have you asked long life — but *have asked wisdom and knowledge for yourself* . . . wisdom and knowledge are granted to you; and I will give you riches and wealth and honor, such as none of the kings have had who were before you, nor shall any after you have the like" (2 Chronicles 1:11–12, emphasis added).

A great and familiar example of the wisdom of Solomon was the story of two harlots who both gave birth to sons. The first woman came to Solomon and told him that the other woman's son died in the night and she switched the babies so that the first woman woke up with the dead one. But she knew that this dead child was not hers. So she asked Solomon to help her regain her son.

Solomon in his wisdom said, "Divide the living child in two, and give half to one, and half to the other" (1 Kings 3:25). But the first woman, whose child had been stolen, cried out and begged Solomon to give the child to the other woman and not let him be killed. But the other woman said, "Let him be neither mine nor yours, but divide him" (1 Kings 3:26).

Solomon knew instantly that the woman who cried out to spare the son's life was the real mother. So the king answered and said, "Give the first woman the living child, and by no means kill him; she is his mother" (1 Kings 3:27).

Unfortunately, Solomon did not continue

to seek God's wisdom forever. Over time he became lustful and gave his heart to many foreign wives, knowing that God said not to intermarry with them because they would turn his heart toward their false gods. And that is exactly what happened. His heart was no longer loyal to God, and he did not follow the leading of the Spirit. He did evil in the sight of the Lord, and it was his downfall.

God discloses things. There may come a warning that you need to hear for your protection and the protection of others, and the Holy Spirit will disclose that to you. He may reveal an error in thinking, and the truth will suddenly become crystal clear. He can show you something that is going on that you were completely unaware of, and suddenly you see it. It is revealed to you for your benefit and sometimes the benefit of others. The Bible says, "Surely the Lord GOD does nothing, unless He reveals His secret to His servants the prophets" (Amos 3:7). So if He doesn't reveal it to you, He will reveal it to others for you.

PRAYER POWER
Lord, I thank You for Your Holy Spirit of wisdom and revelation living in me.

Thank You that Your wisdom gives me common sense and the ability to make wise decisions and choices. Thank You that You store up wisdom for the righteous and You are "a shield to those who walk uprightly" (Proverbs 2:7). Thank You that the fear of You is the beginning of wisdom, and the knowledge of You is understanding (Proverbs 9:10).

I pray for wisdom in all things. Thank You that You give wisdom to those who ask You for it (James 1:5). Help me to always seek Your wisdom and not the wisdom of the world. Help me to increase my learning about You and always get wise counsel when I need it (Proverbs 1:5). I pray I will have wisdom that keeps me safe and delivers me from the "way of evil" (Proverbs 2:10–12). Help me to never forsake wisdom so that my "steps will not be hindered" and I will not stumble (Proverbs 4:12). Give me the revelation I need when I need it. Reveal to me the things I need to understand — the secret things only You know and I need to see.

In Jesus' name I pray.

God has revealed them to us through His Spirit. For the Spirit searches all things, yes, the deep things of God.

1 CORINTHIANS 2:10

If any of you lacks wisdom, let him ask of God, who gives to all liberally and without reproach, and it will be given to him.

JAMES 1:5

Led to Be Filled with His Love and Hope

God is love. Therefore, His Spirit *in* us is love. And that means the more we open up to the fresh infilling of the Holy Spirit *in* us, the more we will have a fresh infusion of God's love flowing *through* us.

The Holy Spirit never displays anything less than pure love. If you see someone claiming to move in the Spirit and they do not manifest the love of God, then they are not moving in the Spirit. They are moving in the flesh. That's how you know who is a true believer and who is not. Jesus said we will be known to be His people by the love we have for others.

The Bible says that love never fails (1 Corinthians 13:8). That is, *God's* love never fails. Human love fails all the time. And don't we know it. The Bible also says we are to *pursue* love (1 Corinthians 14:1). That doesn't mean chasing after some man or woman and talking them into loving *us*. It means seeking the God of love and making way for more of His Spirit of love to flow in us. When we do that, it heightens the sense of hope we have in the Lord. "Now hope does not disappoint, because *the love of God has been poured out in our hearts by the Holy Spirit* who was given to us" (Romans 5:5, emphasis added).

We always have reason to hope because of the unfailing, unconditional love of God for us.

Being filled with the Holy Spirit means you have access to the love of God. Opening up to the flow of His love in you opens your heart so that His love can flow through you to others. The love of God then begins to guide and motivate your actions, thoughts, and words so that it forms your character to become more like the Lord. The love of God in you changes everything. It evaporates the negatives and enlarges the positives.

Paul said that it is only faith working through love that accomplishes anything (Galatians 5:6). Everything we do without the love of God flowing in our hearts is meaningless and pointless and doesn't accomplish anything good. That's why we must keep on being filled with the Holy Spirit, so that we are *continuously* being filled with God's love. When you seek a fresh filling of His Spirit in you every day, His love in you changes your heart. Then His love flowing through you to others changes *their* hearts as well.

The Holy Spirit is the channel though which the love of God fills us and flows through us. Jesus and the Holy Spirit are God's greatest gifts of love to us.

I remember being extremely sick and in great pain in a hospital one time. I was there for a number of days and had many visitors who were warm, comforting, and loving. All of them were believers filled with the Spirit of God, as was all of my nursing staff. What a great gift that was. But one day a couple I did not know came to my room, having been sent by a church. They stood out as quite loveless and cold, and it seemed as though they had a duty to perform and wanted to get it over with. There were a few other people visiting me at the time, and they noticed it too. I wanted to cheer them up by telling them of how God had saved my life, but the man interrupted me and said, "Don't talk! We're here to pray and we have other people to see." I felt bad for the other people they were going to see because unless their relationship with God was very strong, a visit with this couple was not going to help them.

If we are not motivated by the love of God in our heart, then even the good things we do accomplish little or nothing. "Though I bestow all my goods to feed the poor . . . but have not love, it profits me nothing" (1 Corinthians 13:3). I certainly don't want to seem at all ungrateful for that couple's effort to come to the hospital, but the encounter was more sad than uplifting. It was in stark contrast to the others who came, motivated by the love of God poured out by His Holy Spirit.

The answer to everything we do in life is the love of God. We need more love than we are capable of generating on our own. We need greater hope in our lives than what we can ever conjure up or talk ourselves into. Without *God's* love, and the hope we have in Him, we can never achieve His peace that passes all understanding.

Because of His unfailing love for us, we always have hope. God's love in full measure flowing through us by the Holy Spirit points us to our hope. In fact, we can overflow with hope because of the Holy Spirit in us (Romans 15:13). Our hope is in Jesus (Colossians 1:27). The hope we have in the Lord is "an anchor of the soul, both sure and steadfast" (Hebrews 6:19). We will never be disappointed by putting our hope in Him because He proved His love for us on the cross and now by His Holy Spirit in us.

PRAYER POWER

Lord, I worship You and thank You for Your love toward me. Thank You for Your Spirit of love dwelling in my heart so that I am grounded in Your love (Ephesians 3:16–17). Help me to comprehend the width, length, depth, and height of Your love (Ephesians 3:18). Enable me to continuously receive the love of Christ which passes all understanding so that I may be filled with all the fullness of God (Ephesians 3:19).

I open up my heart to receive more of the flow of Your love filling my life. I daily surrender myself to You and ask that You penetrate my mind, emotions, and heart with Your love in ever-deepening ways. Help me to be led and controlled by Your Spirit every hour of every day. Teach me of Your amazing love so that I can see how to love others the way You do. Help me to see every person from the perspective of Your love for them.

I know that though I speak like an angel, but I don't have love, I'm just making noise; and if I have the faith to move a mountain but I don't have love, "I am nothing" (1 Corinthians 13:1–2). I pray Your Spirit of love will flow powerfully through me at all times. Help me to be motivated by Your love in everything I do so that it accomplishes what You want it to.

In Jesus' name I pray.

WORD POWER

Walk in love, as Christ also has loved us and given Himself for us, an offering and a sacrifice to God for a sweet-smelling aroma.

EPHESIANS 5:2

May the God of hope fill you with all joy and peace in believing, that you may abound in hope by the power of the Holy Spirit.

ROMANS 15:13

3
LED TO HEAR

God communicates with us. That's because He is not a cold and distant God who cannot be known. He *wants* us to know Him. And He desires that we hear Him speaking to us through His Word as well as when we pray and worship Him. That's why His Holy Spirit in you will always be leading you to listen for God's voice to your heart.

Early on in my walk with the Lord, Pastor Jack told me, "Don't let where you are become a prophecy of where you are going to stay." I never forgot that. I can still hear his voice in my mind saying those words, and in my heart because of the impact they had on my life.

You have probably had the same experience, when someone has told you something you needed to hear — a warning, perhaps, or needed advice — and you remember that person's voice. You can still hear them speaking those words to you in your mind.

That's what it is like to hear the voice of God speaking to your heart. You don't necessarily hear an audible voice — although that is possible, but not likely. Actually, you don't want to hear God's full voice because from what I understand in Scripture it is frightening.

I remember working at my desk in my office on the second floor of our house in California. The desk was under a large window, and I sat facing that window looking out over the front yard to the street we lived on. As I was writing, I heard the sound of a roaring engine. I looked up and saw an enormous fighter jet speeding straight toward me, flying very low. The closer it came the louder it got, until the noise became engulfing. I thought it would pull up but it didn't, and it looked as if it was barely going to make it over our house. The noise became unbearably loud, and there wasn't enough time to run to a place where there were no windows, so I ducked under my desk in case the glass shattered as the jet passed directly overhead. The noise went through my body and shook my bones. It was beyond frightening. I immediately called the airport and reported it, and they said there had been an air show nearby and this plane had taken off from it but was flying too low. They said they had already received many complaints about it.

Judging by the Old Testament, that is the way I imagine the voice of God would sound if He were to actually speak to us. I'm thinking we should be very thankful for that still small voice of His Spirit in us.

In order to follow the leading of the Holy Spirit, you must hear from God, and you cannot hear from God reliably if you don't have the solid foundation of His Word by which to judge what you are hearing.

When you become so familiar with God's Word that you hear it in your mind and He speaks to you from Scripture, then you will begin to hear His voice speaking to your heart at other times. There will also be promptings to *your* spirit by *His* Spirit, and you will learn to identify them as such. Hearing God communicate to you in these ways guides you in your walk with Him and helps you understand His will for your life.

Led to Hear God's Word in Your Mind

If you are flying a plane, you must be able to read and trust the instrument panel. The air around you can become foggy. Weather patterns can hinder visibility and control so you can't see clearly. You won't always be able to tell exactly where you are headed, and you cannot rely on feelings. Outside influences can bring you down, and you can crash.

The same is true for your life. In order for you to fly on a steady course in the right direction, above or around the dangers in your life, you must have full knowledge and understanding of the flight plan and the instrument panel. The Bible is your instrument panel and gives you your basic flight plan. You must not only know how to read and understand it, you must also learn to trust and follow it explicitly. It will guide you safely where you need to go without crashing.

It's amazing how when you receive the Lord into your life and are filled with the Holy Spirit, God's Word comes alive to your understanding. It makes sense like never before. It affects you positively in every way. It strengthens you. It makes your crooked places straight and causes you to walk on solid ground. The more you read the Bible, the more the Holy Spirit speaks to your heart about it. The more you hear it being taught, the better you will retain it. The more you understand it and etch it in your mind, the better you will be able to have it ready in your heart.

As you learn about God's ways, the Holy

Spirit will put a greater desire in you to live His way. The more you live God's way, the more you will stay on course and end up where you are supposed to be.

Every time you read the Bible, the Holy Spirit in you will teach you new things or give you a deeper understanding about the same things. You should always be able to take away something for you personally. Your eyes will be opened to some new level of what you are reading every time. He will bring to life a particular verse you may have looked at a hundred times, and yet it will speak to you in a new and personal way. That's why you read it over and over. Because each time you read it, you will have a new level of understanding that you didn't have before. You will learn more about who God is and be better able to hear His voice speaking to you.

You will not be able to hear God speaking to your heart if you don't hear Him speaking to you from His Word first.

Try to read some portion of the Bible every day — even if it is only a few verses. God's Word is alive, and you have to feed your spirit on it in order to grow strong. It is also your instrument panel, remember? You must have an accurate sense of your flight plan. Even if you don't know exactly where you are going, it will help you to know for certain where you should *not* be going.

Every time you read the Bible, you are being changed for the better. Even a single verse can set your heart on the right course for that day. And don't be concerned that you can't do everything perfectly. No one can. That's why Jesus sent the Holy Spirit as your Helper. God has put a holy barometer inside of you — His Holy Spirit — and He will not only *lead* you to the Word and the way of obedience, He will *enable* you to do what it says.

Don't be concerned if you do not fully understand everything you read in it. You are living with the Author after all, and He will teach you more every time you read it. And while you don't have to memorize the Bible, committing some key verses to memory is a good thing to do. The more you say them, the more they sink down deep and become part of you. But even if you memorize the words with your mind, you will still need the Holy Spirit to bring them to life in your heart.

God's laws are a sign of *His* love for *us* because they are for *our* benefit. Our *obedience* to His laws is a sign of *our* love *for* Him. Jesus said, "He who has My commandments and keeps them, it is he who loves Me. And he who loves Me will be loved by My Father, and I will love him and *manifest Myself to him*" (John 14:21, emphasis added). How much do we want Jesus to manifest Himself to us? I say as much as possible. Jesus equated loving Him with keeping His Word. He said when we obey His Word, He and His Father God will make their home with us (John 14:22–23). The more your love grows for God and His Word, the more you will want to do what He says.

Moses — who was strong enough in faith for God to use him to set the Israelites free from bondage in Egypt — did not obey God in one important way. As a result he forfeited the greatest desire of his heart, to enter the Promised Land. Even though Moses prayed that he would be able to cross over the Jordan and see the Promised Land, God said because of his disobedience he would have to remain where he was and die there.

We, too, must obey God in order to move into all He has for us. Sin weakens us and shortens our lives. Obedience makes us stronger and extends our lives. We cannot possess all God has for us unless we are doing all He asks us to do. No matter where you are in your life, God is leading you forward into a new place and time. You can't get to the right place if you don't hear God's voice in His Word and obey it, and you may lose the fulfillment of your greatest desire.

Obedience to God's Word brings great reward; disobedience, or rejection of God's laws, keeps us from moving into all God has for us.

If we don't have God's Word in our mind every day, we will forget it. We're like that. Every day apart from the Word waters it down in our memory. The enemy of our soul comes to steal it away or try to convince us to doubt it. We are too easily drawn away by outside influences. And when things start going well in our lives, we forget what God has spoken to us through Scripture. We are especially vulnerable as we are about to enter into our own promised land of success.

Too often when we don't have to depend on God for everything, we think we don't have to depend on God for anything.

A number of times in the Bible God tells His people to "take careful heed . . . lest you act corruptly" (Deuteronomy 4:15–16). Or, if we don't "take heed," we can forget the covenant we have with God and start worshipping other things, and that can shorten our lives (Deuteronomy 4:23–26). One of the ways we "take heed" of what is happening in our heart is to fill it daily with God's Word. God blesses those who keep His laws. But we won't keep His laws if we don't remember what they are. We have to keep reminding ourselves.

God brought the Israelites "out of Egypt *with His Presence, with His mighty power*" (Deuteronomy 4:37, emphasis added). God has the ability to bring *you* out of anything with His presence and His mighty power too. That's because you have access to both because of the Holy Spirit within you. But if you want to possess all God has for you, you have to obey His commands. And you cannot do that without God's Word in your heart. God wants you convinced that you cannot live by bread alone, but by every word that comes from Him (Matthew 4:4).

When you are being led by the Holy Spirit, it will never be in opposition to the Word of God; it will always be in alignment with what the Scriptures say.

We must have faith in order to please God (Hebrews 11:6). And we can't have strong faith without reading, hearing, knowing, and trusting His Word. The promises of God for you are many, and in order to receive them you must believe in God and what His Word says about them. The same Spirit who inspired the men who wrote the Scriptures will also inspire you and teach you as you read it.

Logos is the whole message — the Bible in its entirety. *Rhema* is a part of the message — the spoken word in communication of the message. It is a verse from the Bible that a believer uses as a weapon in the spiritual battle. You must have both *logos* and *rhema*. That's why you need to read the entire Bible many times over and also know specific verses God quickens to your heart. That will grow your faith to trust completely in the truth of His Word.

God honors those who honor Him by living according to His Word; disobedience to God's laws opens your mind to be taken in by deception.

God wants you to open up to His Spirit working in your life, but you must always view Him from the illumination of Scripture. The Holy Spirit waits for you to release His power by speaking His Word. He waits for you to not only speak it with your mouth, but to also believe it in your heart enough to do it. Ask the Holy Spirit to lead you deeper into His Word than ever before so you can know and recognize His voice speaking to you from it.

God has so much He wants to accomplish through You. God's Word — His instruction book — is specific about what He wants. Take time in the Bible every day, for the hidden things of God are found there.

PRAYER POWER

Lord, I thank You that by the power of Your Spirit You have given me Your Word. I see it is impossible to know *You* without knowing *it.* I ask that Your Holy Spirit, who inspired the writing of the Scriptures, will bring it alive in my mind and my heart every time I read or hear it. Make every verse clear to my understanding so that I have a deeper comprehension of the full meaning of each one. Help me to retain it. Prepare me with Your Word so that I am complete and thoroughly equipped for everything You have for me to do.

Strengthen me with knowledge of Your truth and help me to obey what You have said to do. Teach me what I don't understand. Make Your Word become part of the fabric of my being. Weave it into my soul so that it forms who I am. Illuminate each word and give me knowledge that I could not have on my own. Help me to hear Your voice speaking to me every time I read it. I don't want to be a person who turns my ear away from hearing Your law so that my prayers become an abomination (Proverbs 28:9). I want the peace You have promised to those who love Your ways (Psalm 119:165). Your Word is perfect — changing me, making me wise, bringing me joy, and flooding my life with light (Psalm 19:7–8).

In Jesus' name I pray.

WORD POWER

The word of God is living and powerful, and sharper than any two-edged sword, piercing even to the division of soul and spirit, and of joints and marrow, and is a discerner of the thoughts and intents of the heart.

HEBREWS 4:12

All Scripture is given by inspiration of God, and is profitable for doctrine, for reproof, for correction, for instruction in righteousness.

2 TIMOTHY 3:16

Led to Hear God's Voice to Your Heart

The more you put God's Word into your mind, the more you will hear God's voice speaking to your heart. He will never lead you in any way that does not totally line up with His Scriptures.

God is very specific. When He gave Moses instructions with regard to the offerings, feasts, Sabbaths, care of the tabernacle, rituals for cleansing, regulations for the priests, and much more, He gave very specific instructions. Everyone knew exactly what they were to do, as well as what they were *not* to do. Nothing was ever left to chance. God gave the promise of blessing if they obeyed and the promise of retribution if they did not (Leviticus 26).

God is also very specific about the things He wants you to do, and *not* do, in your own life. That's why He will speak to your heart about specific things that are relevant to your individual situation, the specifics of which are not literally mentioned in the Bible. For example, He doesn't tell you specifically in His Word which job you are to take or what house you should buy, but He will speak to your heart about it when you pray and ask Him to show you.

The more you hear God's voice in His Word, the more you will recognize the voice of His

Spirit speaking to you as you pray for His leading.

God promised Joshua He would drive out the enemy in Jericho, but they had to do as God *specifically* instructed them to do (Joshua 6:1–5). So the Israelites walked around Jericho seven times, just as God said, and on the seventh time the people shouted when they heard the priests blow the trumpets. Then the enormous wall surrounding Jericho fell down flat and the people took the city (Joshua 6:20). The walls fell down because the Israelites obeyed a word from God. God had instructed them *specifically* as to what they were to do. (In case you are the sensitive type and were concerned for the people in Jericho who lost their walls and much more, this was a move of God in order to bring judgment upon that corrupt city. So don't feel bad for them.)

God is specific, and if we want success in our personal lives, we must listen to what the Holy Spirit specifically tells us to do.

Josiah was one of Judah's greatest kings. He followed the law of God and brought about great reforms. He was steady in seeking the Lord and purging the land of false gods and idols. But he did not hear when God was speaking to him through the king of Egypt. Even though the king warned Josiah that God was with *him* and *not Josiah,* and he should not fight against him, Josiah would not listen. *And he did not seek God about going to war* against the king of Egypt. He fought with him anyway, not recognizing that the king's words were a warning from God (2 Chronicles 35:21–22).

If Josiah had just asked God, he would have had a word in his heart from the Holy Spirit telling him that God was speaking to him through the king and warning him not to go out to fight. But Josiah didn't ask, and as a result he was killed in the battle.

How many times has this same thing happened to us or to people we know? When a warning was given from some person we did not heed and the results were disastrous? How many times has someone you know gotten into serious trouble because they didn't seek a word from the Lord regarding what they were about to do? Or they *did* seek Him, received a warning in their heart, and ignored it? Too often, I'm afraid.

The Bible tells of a prophecy brought by the prophet Joel, which is a promise from God for people in the last days. We are in the last days now, and who can deny it?

What a privilege to watch the events unfolding around the world — as hard as they are to see — telling us that events God has foretold through His Spirit, His Son, and His prophets are now happening. This prophecy says, "It shall come to pass in the last days, says God, that *I will pour out of My Spirit on all flesh; your sons and your daughters shall prophesy,* your young men shall see visions, your old men shall dream dreams . . . and it shall come to pass that *whoever calls on the name of the LORD shall be saved*" (Acts 2:17,21, emphasis added).

This word is for us. We who are believers are all sons and daughters of God. We can expect God to speak to us, and use each of us to speak a word from Him to others. And this is not just for a few special people. It is for everyone. It says "all" people. God may give you a word from Him to speak to someone else. It could be to warn them of something that will happen. Or to tell them what they should or should not be doing. It can often happen when you are praying for that person.

When you have a sense that you have received a word from the Lord for someone else, be sure to seek God about this first, *before* you say anything to anyone else. Be 100 percent certain that what you are sensing is from God and not your own soul. It's not that you cannot have certain strong personal feelings about the situation. It's just that you don't want your own feelings to get in the way of a person being able to recognize that the message is from God and not you. When you share a message with someone that you feel God has spoken to your heart, they need to sense the magnitude of what you are saying — that it is coming from God. Also, make sure that this message is for *you* to tell that person. It may be just for you to *pray* for them regarding it. Don't do anything until you are certain you have heard from God.

Always remember that a word from God to someone else should only be delivered with the love of God in your heart. The attitude should not be, "What you are doing is stupid and I have to stop you." It should be, "I care about you and am concerned, but *more* than that, *God* loves and cares about you and has this message for you." People will always receive a word with a receptive ear if they believe it is from God and delivered with His love.

The times I have had to tell someone something from the Lord, He has emboldened me to say it. And I knew I would never have had peace until I did what He was telling me to do. Nor would I have ever said it on my own. This is not something I normally do. I don't go up to people and tell them things about themselves unless I know with absolute certainty it is from God. When it is the Lord, I know it.

If someone gives you "a word from the Lord," seriously consider the source. Determine whether that person is strong in the Word and led by the Holy Spirit. Don't reject or accept it immediately without asking God to speak to *your* heart about it. We are supposed to test all things and hold fast to what is good (1 Thessalonians 5:21). God may confirm it to your heart right then, or perhaps later on, or perhaps never.

I have had many people give me "a word from the Lord," and I knew it was from God. But there were a couple times when I knew it was not from God because the Spirit in me did not bear witness to it. The "word" was later proven without a doubt to be inaccurate. In every case it was from someone who was spiritually immature. I didn't know them, so I didn't know at the time whether their walk with God was solid — if he or she was a person of the Word who was led by the Holy Spirit.

The first time it happened I was a fairly new believer and pregnant with my first child. A young woman in church near where I was sitting gave me a "word from God" that I was going to have a girl. However, I had clearly heard God's voice to my heart months earlier that I was going to give birth to a boy and we were to call his name Christopher. We had already picked out another name, so we changed it. Her word made me sad because it caused me to momentarily doubt that I had actually heard from God. But when I prayed about it later, I knew I had certainly heard from God. After that, I never doubted it for a moment. A few months later our son was born.

The young woman later apologized to me for rushing ahead with a word without confirming it with the Lord first. I told her there was no harm done because I already knew what I had heard from God as a word to *my* heart. There is a danger in thinking that everything that comes to your mind is from God. It won't be. And you will know without a doubt when it is. If you have any uncertainty whatsoever about whether what you have heard is from God, don't say anything at all.

Ask God to help you hear His voice to your heart so you won't miss what He wants to tell you. Shut out the noise and distractions around you. Ask Him to silence any anxieties within you. God may be wanting to speak to you right now about something very specific.

PRAYER POWER

Lord, help me to hear Your voice speaking to me when I read Your Word so that I can recognize Your voice speaking to my heart at other times as well. I know You care about the details of my life, so I ask You to help me understand when You are giving me specific directions. Keep me from moving on something before I know what You are leading me to do. I don't want to do anything without seeking You first.

There are many things I am unsure about each day, and I cannot navigate through my life without hearing Your voice to my heart telling me which way to go. I know You are specific about the things You want me to do because You want what is best for my life. Help me to walk the right path every day. If there are words you want me to speak to another person, give me the "tongue of the learned" so that I will "know how to speak a word in season to him who is weary" (Isaiah 50:4). Keep me from saying anything to someone in the way of advice or warning that is not of You. If someone speaks a word to me, help me to know for certain whether it is from You or not. Teach me to become good at hearing Your voice and following Your leading in my life.

In Jesus' name I pray.

WORD POWER

Eye has not seen, nor ear heard, nor have entered into the heart of man the things which God has prepared for those who love Him. But God has revealed them to us through His Spirit. For the Spirit searches all things, yes, the deep things of God.

1 CORINTHIANS 2:9–10

Now we have received, not the spirit of the world, but the Spirit who is from God, that we might know the things that have been freely given to us by God.

1 CORINTHIANS 2:12

Led to Hear God's Prompting of Your Spirit

Not long ago I was about to leave my house for an appointment. As I was getting in my car I was prompted by the Holy Spirit to take care of something before I left that I wasn't intending to do right then. It took a few minutes, which made me leave a little later than I was expecting. When I was about five minutes down the narrow two-lane highway I always travel on, I came upon an enormous accident involving at least five cars and perhaps more. They were strung across both lanes with tremendous damage and injuries. It looked to me as though there must have been at least one head-on collision that affected other cars. I had never before seen anything like that on this long stretch of highway. After I got beyond the initial shock, I knew that if I had not gone back to do what God was prompting me to do, I could have been in that accident.

How many people have died or been killed because they either didn't inquire of the Lord about what they were doing, or they did but didn't listen to the Holy Spirit's prompting? Or they were warned about something but did not recognize the Lord speaking to them through someone else? This does not mean that you take every instruction or warning from someone as a word from God. But you should ask God if it *is* or not. Don't *assume* that it isn't. Don't ignore the prompting of the Holy Spirit in your own heart. Too many people do that because they either don't recognize the Holy Spirit speaking to them or they think they know best.

The more time you spend with God reading His Word, praying, and worshipping Him, and the more you obey Him, the more you will hear the Holy Spirit's prompting in your spirit. You will have a sense when something is wrong, even if you don't know exactly what it is. You may not hear a specific instruction, but you will know when you need to leave a place and go someplace else. Or not go at all. Or stop by to see if someone is okay. Or make that phone call. Or change your plans. You will begin to trust the Holy Spirit instructing you and impressing you about specific things.

We who walk with God must be receptive to promptings from the Holy Spirit. A prompting is a nudge from the Holy Spirit. It is not the same as a clear word from Him where you hear the words in your mind and heart. Other words for "prompt" are "inside information," "advice," "a word to the wise," "whisper," "caution," "warning," "signal," "privileged information," and "a strong impression." It is a sense you have about something. And it is Holy Spirit initiated.

I went to a physical therapist for my back a few days before my son's wedding. On my way home I had a prompting I should stop by a certain business to make sure that something very important I needed to pick up for the wedding would be ready on time. I definitely did *not* want to take the time to stop, because I was already late for a dinner party, it had been a busy day, it was going to be inconvenient to stop, I felt quite tired, and also it was painful getting in and out of the car. But I knew I should not ignore the prompting in my spirit that said I should stop to see if everything was on schedule.

I had specifically prayed that day, and every day, for all the wedding details. That's why I thought it must be the Holy Spirit guiding me. If it had been left up to me, I would not have even thought to go there. So I stopped in at this place of business just as they were closing at 6:00 p.m. Another minute later and they would have been gone. I was shocked to find out that they had been so swamped with business that week that what I needed for the wedding had been pushed to the back of their schedule. The owner had completely forgotten the date of the wedding and assumed we had a few weeks more, when actually there were only two days left. If I had not stopped right then and checked on it, what I needed would not have been done.

I thanked God profusely all the way home for that prompting. The Holy Spirit was in the details because I had invited Him to be. He had prompted my heart to do something I didn't want to do, and thank God I listened.

The closer you are to God, the more you welcome the fullness of His Spirit in you, the more you will learn to identify and trust His promptings to your heart.

This has happened countless times to me. I could write an entire book on this subject alone. I am sure these things have happened to you as well if your heart is sensitive to the Holy Spirit. In order to not miss a prompting of your soul by the Holy Spirit, stay close to the Lord and walk with Him in His Word, in prayer, and in praise and worship every day. You will be so glad you did.

PRAYER POWER

Lord, help me to always walk so closely with You that I never fail to recognize the prompting of Your Spirit to my soul. Enable me to not only identify it, but also to never ignore it. Teach me to be

117

so in tune with You that I know right away when it is You prompting me to do something. Help me to trust it and act upon it. Thank You for the many times You have impressed something upon my heart and have spared me much grief and trouble. Teach me to be so solid in Your Word that I hear the voice of Your Spirit speaking to my heart and Your prompting in my soul about the details of my life.

Give me calm and quiet in my spirit so that I can hear You whisper to my soul. I want to listen for Your voice at all times so that I am always sensitive to Your Spirit nudging me. Keep me from becoming dull of hearing so I can stay attuned to Your voice within me. I don't want to be like the people who, when You called, they did not answer, and when You spoke, they did not hear (Isaiah 65:12). Keep me from ever being at a place where I cannot hear Your prompting to my heart.

In Jesus' name I pray.

WORD POWER

He who is of God hears God's words.
JOHN 8:47

Your ears shall hear a word behind you, saying, "This is the way, walk in it," whenever you turn to the right hand or whenever you turn to the left.

ISAIAH 30:21

Led to Hear God's Will for Your Life

The Holy Spirit will always lead you into the will of God for your life. The way you live in God's will is to walk with Him step-by-step and do what you know for sure is the will of God each day. For example, it is always the will of God to worship Him, to pray without ceasing, to be in His Word, and to give thanks. It is always God's will to walk "in the fear of the Lord and in the comfort of the Holy Spirit" (Acts 9:31). When you know you are doing the will of God as clearly expressed in His Word, then the will of God for you personally will unfold.

If you are to find God's will for your future, then you must listen closely for the Spirit's leading as you walk with Him moment by moment today. As you depend on Him for every step, He gets you where you need to go in order to move into the future He has for you.

We never know all the details of our future. Sometimes all we really know is we have one, and that it is good. But we *do* know that the future God has for us is far better than the one we can think of for ourselves, because He said so. Abraham didn't know where he was going when he went out on a journey that God was leading him to take. But he knew that following God's leading and doing His will was the only way to live. So he became one of the biggest success stories of all time. And all he did was faithfully follow the leading of the Lord.

When God directs you to do something by His Spirit speaking to your heart and you say yes to it, you are declaring that you want His will over your own.

Because God has given us a free will, the Holy Spirit will not stop us if we choose *our* will over *His.* But no matter how hard we pray for something that is not His will, He will not give us anything that is going to be bad for us.

David ignored what he knew was God's will. He numbered the fighting men he had with him so he could judge Israel's strength by manpower instead of relying on the Lord's strength as he should have done. He realized that what he had done was a sin against God and flagrantly out of His will (2 Samuel 24:10). God gave David a choice as to what horrible consequence he would endure for his sin. David chose a plague, which killed 70,000 of his men. When we step out of God's will we can be forgiven, but we will still suffer consequences because of it.

Learning to hear the voice of God is crucial to staying in the will of God. And don't think for a moment that it's not possible to hear God. If the devil can tell you to do something wrong, God can certainly tell you to do something right. And the Holy Spirit will give you the ability to know the difference.

Jesus said, "Not everyone who says to Me, 'Lord, Lord,' shall enter the kingdom of heaven, but he who does the will of My Father in heaven" (Matthew 7:21). It is not enough to know Him; we must also live according to His will.

God's promises to us are fulfilled as we follow God and live in His will. When we do, we find the provision, victory, blessings, and rest we need. The more mature we grow in the Lord, the more dependent we are on Him. And that's a good thing. Because we cannot get to where He wants us to go unless we depend entirely on Him to lead us. If we are not following Him, but instead are following the dictates of our own heart, then we are not going to end up where we are supposed to be and we will forfeit the blessings He has for us.

God doesn't keep His will a secret that you must struggle to find out, but He wants you to seek Him for it.

God opens and closes doors in your life. When you seek His will above all else, He will close the door on anything that is not His will for you. If you are not to do a certain thing, you won't have the peace of God about doing it. You will feel uneasy, troubled, or heavy in your heart. If a decision you are about to make *is* God's will, you will have peace and joy concerning it, even though it may be scary if He is leading you to step out in faith in some way. The Holy Spirit "makes intercession for the saints according to the will of God" (Romans 8:27). The Spirit knows the will of God because He *is* God, and He will lead you to pray according to His will. Stay close to Him and you will see.

PRAYER POWER

Lord, help me to hear Your voice speaking to me and giving me direction for my life. Enable me to follow You so closely that I never walk in any kind of rebellion against You. Keep me from being stubbornly addicted to my own desires, wants, or determinations. Teach me to not be concerned with the esteem of men, but to be diligent about pleasing You. Keep me from ever rejecting Your leading. "Teach me to do Your will, for You are my God; Your Spirit is good. Lead me in the land of uprightness" (Psalm 143:10).

I am grateful that Your will for my life is good and it can be known. Give me wisdom to understand what Your will is (Ephesians 5:17). Enable me to do it. Help me to pray according to Your will, because I know You especially hear those prayers (1 John 5:14–15). I choose to surrender to Your will every day so that I never get off the path You have for me. Lead me, Holy Spirit, to do what's right in every situation. Line up my heart with Yours. Help me to clearly hear Your leading so that I am always in Your will. Enable me to be fully available to do what You want me to do so that I can accomplish Your will for my life and Your will in this world. "I delight to do Your will" each day (Psalm 40:8).

In Jesus' name I pray.

Do not be unwise, but understand what the will of the Lord is.

EPHESIANS 5:17

As you have always obeyed, not as in my presence only, but now much more in my absence, work out your own salvation with fear and trembling; for it is God who works in you both to will and to do for His good pleasure.

PHILIPPIANS 2:12–13

4
LED TO WORSHIP HIM

I never knew what joy was until I first experienced it in worship. The joy of the Lord came into my soul like a sunrise, flooding the dark places of my heart with light and melting the hard, frozen areas like ice cubes on a warm day. Tears flowed without effort like a soft summer rain out of my weary soul, and something in me released and I was changed. I felt it. I knew it. I have never gotten over that. And it happened every time I was in a worship service there at the church.

That manifestation of the presence of God cannot be obtained by a formula or some kind of manipulation. It only happens when we have a heart of deep love and reverence for God and we take delight in expressing that to Him. It happens when we turn our eyes completely on Him, exalting God for who He is and praising Jesus for what He has done. It happens when like-minded people gather together with hearts united in love for the Lord and invite the Holy Spirit to move in power through them.

It was always a miracle to me how God would change *my* heart every time I worshipped *Him*. He will do that with anyone who lets go of himself to focus entirely on Him. I love that about God — the thing that is all about *Him* turns out to be for *our greatest blessing.*

When your worship is all about God, He pours Himself into you. In fact, there are certain blessings He wants to give you that you can only receive when you are worshipping Him.

The Holy Spirit will always lead you to worship God, but He doesn't demand it; He inspires it. This is not some mind-control thing where the cult leader wants you to worship him. God is not insecure and needs to be told how great He is. Worship is full recognition of what is the ultimate truth — that God is the almighty, all-powerful Creator of all, the heavenly Father of love, grace, and mercy, and that His Son, Jesus, laid down His life for us and was resurrected to prove that He is God and we can be resurrected too.

The better you know God, the more you will want to worship Him. And every time you worship Him, you know Him better. If you understand who God really is, you cannot stop yourself from worshipping Him.

Your worship determines in whose image you will be formed. You become more like the Lord as you worship Him.

Worship must become a way of life — something that happens countless times a day, every day. It's not just an infrequent thing that happens only on Sunday morning or Wednesday night. It must be continuous and ongoing, like the air we breathe. *The only way to keep worship alive in our hearts is to make it a lifestyle.* The Holy Spirit helps you to do that. He will lead you to worship God anytime it is in your heart and mind to do so.

You cannot be close to God if you don't worship Him. And if you don't worship Him daily, you will never be as close to Him as you can be. You are the closest to God you are able to be on this earth when you worship Him, because He dwells in your praises (Psalm 22:3).

When we praise God for who He is, we begin to better understand who we are in relation to Him.

We make decisions every day about who and what we will worship. Because God

127

gave us a free will — instead of making us robots that He can program to worship Him — we can *choose* to worship *Him.* We set the course of our life by whom or what we worship, because that determines our priorities and values. God wants us to worship Him with our whole heart, in spirit as we are Holy Spirit enabled, and with the truth He has given us.

Led to Worship Him with Your Whole Heart

God wants us to love Him with all our heart, soul, and mind. He said, "You will seek Me and find Me, when you search for Me *with all your heart*" (Jeremiah 29:13, emphasis added). And that's the way we are to worship Him too. The most important thing we do on this earth is worship God.

You were born to glorify God, and the most significant way to do that is to worship Him.

As we pour ourselves out in worship of Him, He pours Himself into us. As you open your heart to Him in praise, He enlarges your heart's capacity to receive His love, peace, joy, and power. As you let the joy of the Lord rise in your heart, it crowds out fear, anxiety, and doubt. As you set your mind to focus on Him, He takes away confusion and gives you clarity. As you set

128

aside your weariness and cares and worship Him, He renews, refreshes, enlightens, and frees you from whatever has restricted you. As you offer to Him all that is within you, He fills you with Himself and fulfills your need for intimacy. As you lift your hands and heart to Him, He lifts you above the circumstances that concern you. As you break your silence and worship Him aloud, He breaks the chains that imprison you.

Worship is speaking all the reasons God is worthy of being exalted. If you don't know where to start, let me give you some ideas. ✓ Praise God as your Creator and heavenly Father, who loves you unconditionally and forever. Praise Jesus that He laid down His life for you so that you can live in complete forgiveness and have a glorious, safe refuge eternally with Him in heaven. Praise Him that He saves, redeems, heals, provides, protects, and delivers you. Worship Him because He has given you His Holy Spirit to live in you and work through you. Praise God that His Word provides a solid foundation for you and is a love letter from Him to read throughout your life. Praise God for His goodness. Worship Him because He is all-powerful. Praise Him because He is the same yesterday, today, and forever. Worship Him who is the unfailing light in this world of darkness. Praise Him that He has a great purpose for you, and that He is always with you and will never forsake you.

Start there!

If all that doesn't stir something in your heart, then start with the basics — the fact that God has given you life, you woke up this morning, and you didn't die in the night.

Worship is responding to God's greatness by exalting Him, but you won't exalt Him as you should if you don't fully understand how great He is.

God wants your worship to be personal. He absolutely wants you to worship Him along with other believers, but He also desires that you worship alone — just you and Him. God also requires that your worship of Him not be just with your lips. He wants it to come from your *whole* heart. Jesus said, "This people honors Me with their lips, but their heart is far from Me. And in vain they worship Me, teaching as doctrines the commandments of men" (Mark 7:6–7). He was quoting Isaiah's words from hundreds of years before, and like Isaiah, Jesus did not validate the worship of people who spoke words of praise but their hearts weren't in it. True worship flows from our heart, or else we are hypocrites.

If we are just going through the motions, singing or reciting words we've heard, we are just acting or following a dead tradition. We are called to worship God with genuine praise that flows out of our heart. Worship should not have to be *pulled* out of us. We should have so much gratefulness and reverence for God that we can't stop it from flowing out.

But if, for some reason, we cannot bring ourselves to worship God, then we have heart problems. I'm not saying you can't start by speaking or singing words of praise whether your heart is in it or not, because once you get started, your heart will come along. If you find yourself unable to worship God because of hurt, depression, anger, unforgiveness, or whatever lies the enemy has told you, you can break through that paralysis by deliberately saying, "Father God, I worship You above all else. Jesus, You are Lord of heaven and earth, and I praise You for saving and delivering me." Then make yourself sing a song of worship, even if you don't feel it at the moment. That is not hypocrisy. That's resisting the enemy.

A hypocrite is someone who goes through ritual motions with no feeling behind it as a show for others. A person who is trying to break through a wall of discouragement or pain, erected by the enemy of their soul due to circumstances, is not a hypocrite for speaking words of praise and worship, even though they don't feel it in their heart at the moment. If you have trouble doing even that, then put on worship music and play it loud enough to drown out the voices of negativity in your head. Worship is powerful, and it will break through anything. Sing along with it. Start by humming along if that is all you are able to do. Don't do nothing. Ask the Holy Spirit to lead you.

In worship we lift our hearts and hands toward heaven and let go of everything on earth.

The greatest evidence of our love and devotion for God is our worship of Him. Worship means that all the focus is on *Him.* It's not on us, or those around us, or the worship leader, or the people on the worship team. God wants to give you a garment of praise for a spirit of heaviness. And that's a perfect trade.

Godly King Josiah restored the worship of God by first of all *reading the Word of God out loud* to the priests and the people (2 Kings 23:2). Then he committed to follow God and keep His commandments *"with all his heart and all his soul"* (2 Kings 23:3, emphasis added). Right away he destroyed all that was unholy in the land. He cleansed the temple of everything used in the worship of false gods and idols (2 Kings 23:4). He tore down the high places that the other kings before him had not done and removed the priests who practiced idol worship (2 Kings 23:8). It is said of Josiah that "there was no king like him, *who turned to the LORD with all his heart, with all his soul, and with all his might"* (2 Kings 23:25, emphasis added).

We, too, must tear down the high places in our heart and destroy anything unholy in our lives. We, too, must get rid of every false god and idol, and get free of any person in our lives who is an evil influence. We must ask the Holy Spirit to cleanse our hearts of everything that is not of Him so that we can turn to God in worship with all our heart, soul, and strength.

King David and the people of Israel accompanied the ark of God back to Jerusalem from where it was in the days of Saul. They put it on a new cart and worshipped God with *"all their might"* as they traveled with it (1 Chronicles 13:8, emphasis added). In fact, the people *stopped often* to worship. "So it was, when those bearing the ark of the LORD *had gone six paces,* that he sacrificed oxen and fatted sheep. Then David danced before the LORD with all his might . . . So David and all the house of Israel brought up the ark of the LORD with shouting and with the sound of the trumpet" (2 Samuel 6:13–15, emphasis added).

We, too, must stop often to worship God with all our might.

When we do not worship God, we are taking God off His throne in our heart and putting ourselves on the throne of our own kingdom in our own world. That's what Lucifer did before he fell from heaven and became Satan on earth. He was a beautiful being — the leader of worship in heaven — but he wanted to be God. We want nothing to do with his pride and failure.

When King David bought a place to build an altar to the Lord to present offerings to Him, he said that he would not "offer burnt offerings to the LORD my God with *that which costs me nothing*" (2 Samuel 24:24, emphasis added). As a result, the Lord heeded his prayers for the land and a plague was stopped in Israel (2 Samuel 24:25). We cannot worship God with limp, lifeless, effortless praise that costs us nothing. We must sacrifice all that is within us — body, mind, and soul. That means we must make a good effort.

134

When we worship things that cannot save us or give us life, we become dead like they are. Every time we worship God for who *He* is, He infuses us with His life-changing power. It softens our heart and makes us strong. He gives us His joy to rise up in our heart and become strength to us.

Our worship affects who we are, because we become like who or what we worship (Psalm 115:4–8).

When the people who had been taken away captive returned to Jerusalem to rebuild the temple, the first thing they did was to build the altar and restore worship. When the foundation of the temple was laid, the people praised God and "shouted with a great shout" (Ezra 3:11). The word for shout means *"a great noise that cannot be ignored."* That sums up the way we should praise God at times. We must praise Him quietly and reverently too, but there have to be times when we sing or speak praise to God with a sound that cannot be ignored.

Even though this verse in Ezra is talking about restoring the temple that had been decimated, we can also compare it to our own lives and the places where we need

God to restore a dead or damaged part of our mind, heart, or memory that has been perverted from the way God intended for it to be. Restoration of any kind should bring shouts of praise and tears of joy, as it did for the people in Jerusalem who saw the restoration of their beloved temple of God that had been destroyed.

Whether it is in the privacy of your own room or in the midst of worship with a congregation, sing out and speak words of praise in your worship time. Simply speaking or singing audibly will be a step forward for many people. This is not about being out of order or attracting attention to yourself. This is about exalting God so the enemy will hear it. Praise is a weapon of warfare. This is not about volume. It is about what's in your heart.

It's not hard to find reasons to praise God, but it can be hard to make ourselves worship Him as often and as wholeheartedly as we should. That is why we need to be fully led by the Holy Spirit. He will always lead us toward worship. It is *you* who determines how much of your heart goes into it. He wants you to worship Him because that positions you to be able to receive all the blessings He has for you.

PRAYER POWER

Lord, I don't ever want to be a weak, ineffective, or halfhearted worshipper of You. You are everything to me. I don't want to be like the people in Your Word who had it all — Your presence and Your Holy Spirit with them — and they lost it. They had the most valuable and precious gift in life, and they wasted it because their hearts were far from You. They started out as grateful worshippers and ended up being ravaged without Your presence to protect them. Keep me far from that. Teach me to worship You with my whole heart. Remind me to combat the difficulties in my life with worship because You are far greater than anything I face.

I don't want my worship to ever reflect anything but total and true reverence for You. Forgive me for any time I have not given thanks to You as I should have. Teach me how to worship You with my whole heart — with everything that is in me. "My soul follows close behind You" (Psalm 63:8). Reveal to me anything in my heart that holds back from giving You all the praise and worship You deserve. Help me to make worship of You the first place I run to when I have concerns. Enable me to make it a way of life.

In Jesus' name I pray.

WORD POWER

I will bless the LORD at all times; His praise shall continually be in my mouth.

PSALM 34:1

Now we know that God does not hear sinners; but if anyone is a worshiper of God and does His will, He hears him.

JOHN 9:31

Led to Worship Him with the Holy Spirit's Help

The Holy Spirit helps us to worship God. Jesus said of true worshippers that *"those who worship Him must worship in spirit and truth"* (John 4:24, emphasis added). The Holy Spirit leads us into worship. He stirs it up in our hearts. He shows us how it should be done.

We have the Holy Spirit when we receive Jesus, but we need the special outpouring of the Holy Spirit that gives us access to the same power Jesus had. After Jesus was baptized by John and the Holy Spirit descended upon Him, He was filled with the Holy Spirit, and He now had the *power of* the Spirit and was *"led by the Spirit"* (Luke 4:1, emphasis added). We, too, need the power and leading of the Holy Spirit. God doesn't give something priceless to someone who doesn't want or appreciate it. We must want it.

The Holy Spirit is also referred to in the Bible as the "Spirit of the LORD" (2 Chronicles 20:14), the "Spirit of God" (2 Chronicles 15:1), and "hand of the LORD" (2 Kings 3:15).

The prophet Elisha needed to hear from God, and he knew *that worship is key to that happening.* He asked for a musician to be brought to him. "Then it happened, when the musician played, *that the hand of the LORD came upon him*" (2 Kings 3:15, emphasis added). That means the Holy Spirit came upon Elisha as he worshipped. Our worship prepares our heart to receive from the Lord.

Worship is the key to hearing God. When we worship God, we open ourselves to the flowing of His Holy Spirit in us bringing into our lives the fullness of God's character. When we worship God, His presence is with us in power and we can better hear from Him.

The continuous flow of the Holy Spirit in you will inspire you to worship God, and as a result, you will be better able to hear His voice speaking to your heart.

The Holy Spirit knows the things of God. "What man knows the things of a man except the spirit of the man which is in him? Even so no one knows the things of God except the Spirit of God" (1 Corinthians 2:11). The Holy Spirit knows how we are supposed to worship Him. When we worship God, we open our whole hearts to Him, and the Holy Spirit is the open channel through which God pours Himself into us. He pours into us His love, joy, peace, power, and all that He is. In that way, He shares Himself with us.

The Holy Spirit — the seal of God's approval of you — enables you to have an ever-deepening relationship with God. The Holy Spirit guides you not only when you pray, but also when you worship Him. He is your source of power so you can accomplish what you could never do without Him. He gives your life meaning and purpose. He illuminates God's Word. He guides you every step of your walk with God.

The Holy Spirit never leads us to complain; He leads us to worship. In fact, if you find yourself complaining, then you are not being led by the Spirit and you need to change that. Complaining is not the same as going before God in prayer and telling Him the concerns of your heart. In prayer you are seeking the Lord's perspective, understanding, wisdom, and help. Complaining about a situation is something you do *instead* of taking your concerns to God. You cannot worship with your whole heart if you are complaining and grumbling.

The Israelites complained against Moses saying, "Why have you brought us up out of Egypt to die in the wilderness? For there is no food and no water, and our soul loathes this worthless bread" (Numbers 21:5). This means they were actually complaining against God. They didn't go to God and humbly say, "Praise You, Lord, that You are our Provider. We worship You as our Almighty God, for whom nothing is impossible. We pray that You will continue to provide the food and water we need."

God wanted them to depend on Him for all their needs because He was going to take them to a place they could not get to without Him. However, as a result of their complaining He "sent fiery serpents among the people, and they bit the people; and many of the people of Israel died" (Numbers 21:6). Isn't it amazing how an

141

invasion of fiery serpents has a way of bringing people back to their senses? So they repented of their complaining and asked Moses to pray that God would "take away the serpents" (Numbers 21:7).

This terrible plague of serpents was the result of complaining and murmuring against God. The people complained instead of worshipped. But God responded to their *confession* and *repentance* by instructing Moses to make a bronze serpent set upon a pole, so that anyone who was bitten could look at it and live. He could have just taken away all the serpents, but instead He provided a way to be saved.

Jesus spoke about this bronze serpent being lifted up in the wilderness and compared it to when He would be lifted up on the cross so "that whoever believes in Him should not perish but have eternal life" (John 3:14–15). Instead of complaining, look to Jesus and the cross, and thank God that He has the way out — or through — everything that concerns you.

When we complain, it always comes back to bite us. Better to thank God for His Spirit in us, guiding us in all things, and that includes worship.

Lord, I thank You for the gift of Your Holy Spirit in me. I value it above all else. Help me to continually be aware of Your presence leading me to worship You. I know You always hear my thoughts, so keep me from allowing ungodly thoughts to steal my mind away. I confess any times I have complained instead of taking my struggles and disappointments to You in prayer. I don't ever want to put my desires before You in any way.

Holy Spirit, I know You can give me words to say (Luke 12:12), You teach me all things (John 14:26), and You can help me do the right thing (Romans 7:6). So I know You will help me to worship You in spirit because You are God's Spirit in me. Cleanse me of all ungodliness so that I am a pure vessel who can worship You in the holiness to which You have called me. Take away anything in my attitude or mind that is not the way You want me to be. I exalt You as the Spirit of life (Romans 8:2) and the Spirit of holiness (Romans 1:4). Enable me to worship You in every way that is acceptable to You.

In Jesus' name I pray.

In everything give thanks; for this is the will of God in Christ Jesus for you.

1 THESSALONIANS 5:18

Who is like You, O LORD, among the gods? Who is like You, glorious in holiness, fearful in praises, doing wonders?

EXODUS 15:11

Led to Worship Him with Knowledge of the Truth

The Holy Spirit is the Spirit of truth. And He wants us to worship Him in the truth of His Word. Before He was crucified, Jesus talked about the Helper whom He would send, "*the Spirit of truth* who proceeds from the Father, He will testify of Me" (John 15:26, emphasis added). The Holy Spirit of truth guides us in all things (John 16:13). He is the Helper who teaches us (John 14:26). He will teach us to worship Him the way He wants to be worshipped.

The Holy Spirit is the presence of God. We cannot actually see God and live, so He gives us His Holy Spirit, who is omnipresent. The work of the Holy Spirit is to fill us with all that God gives us, to empower us to obey Him, and to enable us to do what we could not do without Him.

When we fill our heart with God's Word, it reminds us of who God is and all He has done for us. It causes us to remember what Jesus accomplished on the cross. It teaches us about everything the Holy Spirit is doing in our lives. All this leads us to worship Him in truth.

When the Israelites came into the land they were to possess, they had to totally destroy all the places of idolatry and worship of false gods (Deuteronomy 12:2–4). They were not to incorporate them into their own place of worship. They were to seek the leading of the Holy Spirit to find out what God wanted them to do. We must do the same. We cannot do whatever seems right in our own eyes (Deuteronomy 12:8). We must worship God in the manner He says to worship Him. That is, we must know the truth about how we are to worship God as is revealed in His Word.

Ask God where you are to worship Him with other believers. There are blessings that happen in corporate worship that will not happen any other way in your life. God said, "Take heed to yourself that you do not offer your burnt offerings in every place that you see; *but in the place which the LORD chooses"* (Deuteronomy 12:13–14, emphasis added). Do not attend regular worship services in just any place you see, but in the place God shows you by the leading of His Spirit. That doesn't mean you can't visit other churches, but don't run from place to place, never settling in at a church home.

God has a place for you to worship Him and grow with a church family. Find out where it is. Pray about it. If you are not sure, choose a good church and see if you have the peace of God about attending there. Ask the Holy Spirit to lead you. Don't go to a church where worship is not a priority. Or where it is all frenzy on the platform but nothing is happening in the congregation. Go where there are worship *leaders,* who *lead* the people in worship and not just to do a show for others. This is not about musical styles or volume. It's about everyone putting the entire focus on the Lord and off of themselves. You should be *taught* to worship, not entertained while others worship for you.

Without God's Word illuminating our lives, we will be more persuaded by the world than we are by God.

God gave us His Word so that we would

know how to live — and that includes how to worship. He has rules so that we will know how to make our life work and be able to avoid things that will hurt us. He wants us to know the truth. About everything.

The ultimate truth is God's Word, which is unfailing, dependable, and absolute, and in it you will find everything you need to know about how and why you are to worship Him.

Every time you read the Bible, make a note of the names and descriptions of God as they appear. They will help you to honor Him for who He is. For example, when you read that God is referred to as Heavenly Father, Bread of Life, All-Knowing, Light of the World, Lord of lords, King of kings, Stronghold in the Day of Trouble, Resting Place, Refuge from the Storm, Shade from the Heat, Rewarder, Shield, Sustainer, and Merciful, thank Him that He is these things to *you.* Any one of these is cause for praise. Praise Him because He loves you, He is good, He is pure and holy, He has a purpose for your life, He redeems all things, He hears your prayers and answers them, He never leaves or forsakes you, He can be found by you when you seek Him, He has a high purpose for you, and He is more powerful than anything you will ever face.

Each of these things is found in the Word of God.

You have to know the truth about Jesus. He *is* the truth. When you see Jesus as your Counselor, Savior, Mighty God, Deliverer, Healer, and Prince of Peace, how can you not worship Him (Isaiah 9:6)? When you remember that Jesus made it possible for you to pray in His name and expect to have the joy of answered prayer, you will worship Him (John 16:23–24). When you think of all Jesus has done for you, you will worship Him. I am convinced of that.

PRAYER POWER

Lord, I thank You for the truth of Your Word that shows me how to live. Help me to learn from it how to worship You in ways that please You. I praise You for forgiving me and making it possible for me to have a relationship with You forever. I exalt You, Jesus, and thank You that You rose from the dead and broke the power of death and hell forever in my life. Thank You for saving me from myself and making me alive in You. Thank You that You are growing me into a whole person.

I praise You, Lord, for the gift of Your Holy Spirit in me. I praise You, Holy

Spirit, for guiding me in all things. I know that "Your righteousness is an everlasting righteousness, and Your law is truth" (Psalm 119:142). "I will worship toward Your holy temple, and praise Your name for Your lovingkindness and Your truth; for You have magnified Your word above all Your name" (Psalm 138:2). Because You are at my right hand, I shall not be moved (Psalm 16:8). Help me to daily enter Your gates with thanksgiving and Your courts with praise (Psalm 100:4). Enable me to make worship of You a way of life — my first reaction to all that happens, whether good or bad.

In Jesus' name I pray.

WORD POWER

The hour is coming, and now is, when the true worshipers will worship the Father in spirit and truth; for the Father is seeking such to worship Him.

JOHN 4:23

You are a chosen generation, a royal priesthood, a holy nation, His own special people, that you may proclaim the praises of Him who called you out of darkness into His marvelous light.

5
LED TO BE SEPARATE

We who have the Holy Spirit in us should be different from those who do not. If people cannot see or sense a positive difference in us, then we are not being led by the Spirit in all we do.

The Bible says, "Do not grieve the Holy Spirit of God, *by whom you were sealed* for the day of redemption" (Ephesians 4:30, emphasis added). To "seal" something is to secure and confirm a bond, to give approval of and endorse, and to make it forever binding. Don't you love that this is exactly what Jesus did for your relationship with Him by giving you the Holy Spirit? When you received Jesus, He gave you the Holy Spirit to live in you as *the seal that confirms and secures that bond between you and God* and makes it binding from His standpoint. The Spirit of God is forever committed to reside in you. Does it get any better than that?

The Holy Spirit only *manifests* Himself in

your life, however, as you give place to Him. He will never manifest Himself in any way at all if you don't want Him to. So you can make sure that other people never even suspect He is there. But why restrain the Holy Spirit from doing what He wants to do in you? Why keep Him a secret from others? I don't mean you have to broadcast Him with a megaphone wherever you go. (And we all would rather you didn't.) But why deliberately suppress the Holy Spirit in you when He could manifest the love, peace, and joy of God and draw people to Himself?

We grieve the Holy Spirit when we think, say, or do things that are not holy the way He is holy. When we commit sin in our actions, words, or thoughts — such as when we are unforgiving toward another — the Holy Spirit is grieved, just as you would be grieved if one of your children refused to forgive another of your children. You would have grief over that until it was made right. However, if we are led by the Spirit in all things, we will never grieve Him.

The Holy Spirit will always lead you to become more and more like the Lord. God knows we cannot do that without His enablement. "The flesh lusts against the Spirit, and the Spirit against the flesh; and these are contrary to one another, so that you do not do the things that you wish" (Galatians 5:17).

There you have it. Our flesh, if left to its own way, will be in opposition to the Holy Spirit in us. Either we are submitted to God and the leading of His Spirit or we are not. Either we who are Christ's "have crucified the flesh with its passions and desires" or we have not (Galatians 5:24).

In order for others to see the beauty of God's Spirit in us, we must separate ourselves from all that is not of God.

We can *choose* to separate ourselves from all sin, from the unholy enticement of the world, from the traps and evil plans of the enemy, from all temptation, from the failures of our past, from pride, and from anything that draws us away from God. We have a choice in the way we live.

Led to Be Separate from All Sin
The first thing the Holy Spirit will do, after He leads you to the Lord, is lead you away from all sin. That means every place you are missing the high mark God has for you, the Holy Spirit will bring it to your attention. The Israelites were warned, "You shall walk in all the ways which the LORD your God has commanded you, *that you may live* and

that it may be well with you, and *that you may prolong your days* in the land which you shall possess" (Deuteronomy 5:33, emphasis added).

That's what we want — to live well and long. The Holy Spirit will convict us of any thought, word, or action that keeps us from doing that. And that is why sin is no longer enjoyable — because we sense the Holy Spirit's grief and our own disgust when we do it. The Holy Spirit gives us the power to step away from sin and get free of destructive habits we cannot get free of in our own strength.

Sin separates us from God. The separation happens from *our* side, but we often think it is happening from *God's* side. When we commit a sin, we know it, and if we *don't* come before God immediately in confession with a repentant heart, we allow a wall to go up between us and God. We think *He* is distant, but actually *we* have distanced ourselves from Him by not confessing and repenting of what we've done that violates His laws. "If I regard iniquity in my heart, the Lord will not hear" (Psalm 66:18).

God will not hear our prayers if we continue living apart from His ways.

Sin can creep into our hearts and minds subtly — sometimes without our even realizing it. The truth is, we will always end up living in some way that does not please God when we don't let the Holy Spirit lead us. The Bible says of Rehoboam, one of the kings of Israel, that "he did evil, because *he did not prepare his heart to seek the Lord*" (2 Chronicles 12:14). We have to always aim our heart in the direction of seeking God.

A pattern of action was repeated blatantly over and over in Israel. When things were going well, the people would do evil and forsake God. God would eventually become angry and allow their enemy to defeat and oppress them (Judges 10:6–7). The Israelites would cry out to God, confess and repent of their sin, and He would forgive them. Then the pattern started all over again (Judges 10:10).

God finally got so fed up with their continued sinning that He told the people to go to the gods they had chosen and let *them* save them (Judges 10:14). That's a scary thought. That's like saying, "Let your drugs and alcohol save you." Or, "Let your illicit affair save you." Or, "Let your money save you." Or, "Let your television programs save you." Or, "Let your obsession save you." Or whatever else people worship instead of God.

After that the people of Israel *again* confessed their sins and put away their foreign gods, saying, "We have sinned! Do to us whatever seems best to You; only deliver us this day, we pray" (Judges 10:15). And because God's *"soul could no longer endure the misery of Israel,"* He forgave them (Judges 10:16, emphasis added). God has feelings and He has mercy. He has a soul.

We have a tendency, like the Israelites, to repeat those same patterns in our life unless we are entirely sold out to God. When things are going well, we push the envelope of what we can get away with. Then when things start to fall apart — as they always do — we come back to Him with great repentance. However, every day we are led by the Holy Spirit is a day we can be convicted of sin and put a stop to that pattern of behavior (John 16:8).

If you sin and continue sinning, it doesn't mean the Holy Spirit is not in your life. It means you have not totally surrendered to Him, and you have not listened for His voice leading you every day.

We have to get free of any sin in our lives. And we all have it. "If we say that we have no sin, we deceive ourselves, and the truth is not in us" (1 John 1:8). I have observed people who said they didn't have any sin and were not susceptible to it, and they are the ones who had the greatest fall. Huge! Their pride made them blind to their own fallibility. They fell because they thought they couldn't. And they didn't see the creeping subtlety of sin when it first began encroaching upon their lives. At the point it was no longer subtle, they *refused* to see it. They became so deceived that they established a human justification system they made up for themselves. It can happen to anyone who does not follow the leading of the Holy Spirit.

The Holy Spirit will never lead you to violate His laws. I once heard a man say that he believed the Lord was leading him to leave his wife and marry his already married secretary because she was more in tune with his ministry than his wife was — never mind that his wife's ministry was taking care of their four young children. The leading of the Spirit will never cause you to go against God's ways. Never!

Ask God to make you troubled by sin, because if you continue in sin you will lose your ability to hear the Holy Spirit saying, "Turn back."

Ask the Holy Spirit to reveal any sin in your life *before* He has to convict you of it.

If He reveals something to you, confess and humbly repent of it so you can be forgiven and cleansed. Any sin you give place to — even in your thoughts — will pollute your mind and body and make you miserable anyway, so give it up. It is not worth it.

Any sin in your life grieves the Holy Spirit in you. Just as you wouldn't tolerate a terrible smell in your home, there is a stench of human sin that is intolerable to the Holy Spirit. Don't live with its pollution when you can be cleansed with the sweet aroma of God's forgiveness. Ask the Holy Spirit to give you the strength to free yourself from all sin completely. Ask Him to take away any desire in you for even the thought of it.

Sin kills. But the Spirit in you gives you life (Romans 8:11). God hates sin (Proverbs 8:13). If you love God, you will hate it too. You will hate it enough to separate yourself from it.

PRAYER POWER
Lord, help me to separate myself from all sin. Holy Spirit, I know You lead me away from sin, so I pray I can always hear Your voice speaking to my heart. Give me strong conviction in my soul if I ever hesitate to do the right thing. Keep me from being around anyone or

anything that gives even the appearance of sin. Most of all, I don't ever want to grieve Your Holy Spirit. Keep me from thinking, saying, or doing anything that is in rebellion against Your ways.

Help me to be forgiving and kind to others. I need Your help because I don't always do or say things in a way that pleases You. Enable me to crucify any unholy desires. Give me strength to separate myself from all that is not of You so that I can enjoy a long and good life. I don't want to ever discover a wall of separation between You and me that I have erected because of disregard for Your will and Your ways. I reject all pride in me that even thinks I am incapable of sin. Keep me undeceived about that. Enable me to step away from any desire I have that could keep me from living by Your rules.

In Jesus' name I pray.

WORD POWER

Everyone who has this hope in Him purifies himself, just as He is pure . . . Whoever abides in Him does not sin.

1 JOHN 3:3,6

If we sin willfully after we have received the knowledge of the truth, there no longer remains a sacrifice for sins.

HEBREWS 10:26

Led to Be Separate from the World

God is holy, His Spirit is holy, and He wants us to be holy the way He is. It's not as impossible as it sounds because the Holy Spirit helps us to do it. In fact, there is no way on earth that we can live a life of holiness — which is what being separate from the world is — without His Holy Spirit in us enabling us. It is far too easy to compromise our walk with God by immersing ourselves in attitudes and practices of the unbelieving world around us. We can only be free from those pitfalls when we follow the leading of the Holy Spirit closely.

God made it clear to the Israelites that they should not go after "the gods of the peoples who are all around you . . . lest the anger of the LORD your God be aroused against you" (Deuteronomy 6:14–15). We have to separate ourselves from the worldly attitudes that God hates.

Living separate from the world doesn't mean we become an isolationist and never touch anyone who is not a born-again, Spirit-filled believer. It means we live under

God's control and refuse to be influenced by anything or anyone ungodly. It means we can touch the world with the love of God, yet not be influenced by its practices.

The way you live a holy life is to separate yourself from any transgression of God's ways. Even though the world will try to divert you away from God's purpose for you, reject the counsel of the world and seek the counsel of God. Time and again we read about kings who followed God and did what was right in everything, yet they still did not remove the high places where there was idol worship.

Solomon had it all — prominence, fame, fortune, and the favor of God — but he let the world around him, specifically his many pagan wives, draw him away from God. Solomon was forbidden by God to marry foreign wives, yet he did so anyway. And, just as God had told him would happen, Solomon's heart was led astray by them toward other gods. Eventually, he was no longer loyal to the one true God. Solomon got so far away from following the leading of the Holy Spirit that even after God proclaimed through the prophet Ahijah that He would tear the kingdom away from Solomon, Solomon did not believe him (1

Kings 11:28–32). Because Solomon did not separate himself as God had instructed him, God took his kingdom from him, just as the prophet predicted.

How many times have we lost something valuable that God had for us, all because we did not separate ourselves from the world?

God told the Israelites not to bring anything detestable into their houses. "Nor shall you bring an abomination into your house, lest you be doomed to destruction like it" (Deuteronomy 7:26). We don't want to open the door for destruction in our lives because we have something detestable in our home. Ask God to show you about this. Often we don't think we have anything objectionable to God, but we may have such things as ungodly artifacts, books that exalt sin or other gods, or letters from your old boyfriend or girlfriend before you got married, or whatever else. Look at everything carefully. The Holy Spirit will show you. Whatever you uncover, get rid of it. Completely separate yourself from things that are accursed in the eyes of God.

Living in holiness means that we are to be separated from everything in our lives that is not holy.

■ ■ ■ ■

Moses reminded the Israelites of how the Spirit of God had been with them from the time they left Egypt until they were about to enter the Promised Land 40 years later. He assured them that the Holy Spirit would continue to be with them and guide them if they were obedient to all God instructed them to do. This meant they had to reject whatever the people worshipped in the land they were about to enter.

How many times have we seen certain people whose lives seem full of promise, and they appear to be moving into the promised land of their dreams when something happens to derail everything? My husband and I have seen it too often in the music business where a young and promising artist falls into the pride and idol worship of the culture and doesn't identify the spirit of lust coming to tempt him. After his fall he is never restored to what he was, and certainly not to what he could have been. This is not said with judgment, but rather with heartbreak. What God put in that person in the way of gifts and abilities has been squandered because they did not stay separate from the lure of the world. And now, even though he found forgiveness and restoration, he never shines as brightly. The gifts are still there, but the anointing isn't.

How much better to be led by the Holy Spirit, who will always lead you to be *in* the world but not *of* the world. When you are full of yourself, you are not full of the Spirit. The voice of the Holy Spirit cannot be heard above the world's noise unless we tune out everything else and turn our heart and ears toward Him.

PRAYER POWER

Lord, help me to be separate from the world and yet still be in it in an effective way to do Your will. Show me how to live in this world and be Your light extended without being drawn into and influenced by all that is dark and dangerous to my life. Help me to love unbelievers without being attracted to their self-proclaimed freedom to sin. Strengthen me to reject all peer pressure to be anything other than who You made me to be. Enable me to resist all pride. Keep me undeceived. Help me to never be resistant to what You want to do in my life.

Lord, show me where I have given in to certain practices in the culture I live in that are not pleasing to You. Open my eyes to things I have become accustomed to that I should not have. Help me to shut off or shut down anything that is polluting my mind. Show me if I have brought something into my house that does not glorify You. I don't want anything in my life that would hinder all You have planned for me. Keep me apart from everything that will prevent my prayers from being heard. Holy Spirit, lead me away from the enticement of the world that will only separate me from You.

In Jesus' name I pray.

WORD POWER

Come out from among them and be separate, says the Lord. Do not touch what is unclean, and I will receive you. I will be a Father to you, and you shall be My sons and daughters, says the LORD Almighty.

2 CORINTHIANS 6:17–18

Make confession to the LORD God of your fathers, and do His will; separate yourselves from the peoples of the land.

EZRA 10:11

Led to Be Separate from the Enemy

The Holy Spirit helps us to separate ourselves from the evil around us. When we follow the Holy Spirit, He will lead us away from the traps and pitfalls the enemy sets up for our destruction and help us establish right priorities and good boundaries. In order to destroy the work of the enemy in our lives, we must separate our hearts from his ways and not go panting after his enticements. Ask the Holy Spirit to open your eyes to what is going on around you.

The enemy is a liar, and while you can be opposed to the enemy, you can still be deceived by one of his lies.

The Holy Spirit will always lead us to the truth and reveal deception. Because evil is all around us, we must "walk circumspectly, not as fools but as wise, redeeming the time, because the days are evil" (Ephesians 5:15–16). If we are not wise, we can actually be aiding the enemy in the things we choose to do or support. We must be careful not to join forces with the enemy by supporting his causes and doing his bidding, even if we are unaware of doing that at the time.

Behind every trap of the enemy is a lie he wants you to believe. As illustrated earlier in chapter 2, there is such a thing as a lying spirit, which can *cause* someone to lie (2

Chronicles 18:18–22). The more a person lies, the more a lying spirit is given place. As the lying continues, the person under its influence will lie even when there is no reason for it. They lose all discernment as to what is true and what isn't. They may not even see their lying for what it is, or they may start believing their own lies.

Lying is all too common in the world these days. Too many people lie all the time. Some people are so inundated by a lying spirit that is in the world that they don't know the truth when they hear it. But when you have the Spirit of truth in you, He enables you to discern the truth. He will help you to recognize a lie when you hear it. Someone can be talking to you, and you will know whether he or she is telling you the truth or not.

When you ask the Holy Spirit to show you the truth about something or someone and reveal any lies, He will.

The Nethinim were servants in the temple — janitors, repairmen, woodcutters, water carriers, and maintenance men. Originally they were descendants of the Gibeonites, who were Israel's enemy. However, when the Gibeonites heard what Joshua had done to destroy Jericho, they feared being destroyed by Israel just as the people of Jericho had been. So they cleverly disguised themselves as people from a faraway country who came to make peace with Israel and be their servants (Joshua 9:8). *Joshua did not ask the counsel of God regarding them,* but instead he made a covenant to let them live with them. Later, when Joshua found out they were really his enemies who actually dwelled near them, it was too late because he had already sworn to not touch them (Joshua 9:14–16). So Joshua made them slaves in the house of God (Joshua 9:23–24), which the Nethinim agreed to because it secured their safety.

The Israelites were supposed to be separate from these people, but because Joshua didn't seek the leading of the Lord about them, and instead he believed their lies, the Israelites let the enemy into their midst, which was against God's will for them. It was all part of the people of Israel straying from God's commands, which led to their ultimate downfall.

We must be able to identify our enemy when he comes to us disguised as something else so that we don't invite him into our lives.

Evil forces will join with other evil forces to do evil. The Pharisees and the Herodians were enemies, but they joined together to destroy Jesus (Mark 3:6). Don't be intimidated by a majority, or a crowd, when you are outnumbered. Ask God to show you the truth about the majority around you. Are people intent on evil? Are they doing the enemy's bidding in direct opposition to God? Are they joining forces with others who also want to do evil? Ask the Holy Spirit to show you so that you don't lend your support to people who are on the enemy's side. That can be a very subtle thing, so you need to know the truth about the enemy's plans. Determine to be led by the Spirit of truth.

Satan took Jesus to different places to show Him what He could have if He bowed down to him. But Jesus knew two things:

- He knew the truth about Himself and what His purpose was.
- He knew the truth about Satan and what his plans were.

You need to know those two things as well. Satan will come to you and show you things he says you *should* have or *could* do. But you must remember who you are and what your purpose is and resist him the way Jesus did. You must recognize who Satan is and that his plan for your life is to deceive, rob, kill, and destroy you. You have an adversary who walks around seeking whom he can devour (1 Peter 5:8). Don't let him succeed with you. Be watchful and stay as far away from his territory as you can.

PRAYER POWER

Lord, help me to always recognize the ploys and tactics of the enemy so that I will not aid and abet him in any way. Thank You that You are well able to "deliver me from every evil work" and keep me safe (2 Timothy 4:18). Thank You, Jesus, that You have put the enemy under Your feet. Wherever he tries to erect any kind of stronghold in my life, I pray You will reveal that to me and enable me to separate myself from all of his plans. Keep me from believing any lies of the enemy. Help me to live in truth by standing on the truth of Your Word.

Show me anything I need to see so that I can separate myself from all evil. Show me where I have unknowingly aligned myself with the enemy of my soul. Help me to "abstain from every form of evil" (1 Thessalonians 5:22). Make me aware when I am not as clearly separated from evil the way You want me to be. If the things I am doing, seeing, or saying are supporting the enemy, help me to recognize that and lead me away from it. "I will call upon the LORD, who is worthy to be praised; so shall I be saved from my enemies" (Psalm 18:3). Thank You that You will never leave or forsake me but will always lead me toward You and away from the enemy.

In Jesus' name I pray.

WORD POWER

Be sober, be vigilant; because your adversary the devil walks about like a roaring lion, seeking whom he may devour.

1 PETER 5:8

You who love the LORD, hate evil! He preserves the souls of His saints; He delivers them out of the hand of the wicked.

PSALM 97:10

Led to Be Separate from All Temptation

The Holy Spirit in Jesus enabled Him to resist all temptation, and it is the Holy Spirit in you who will enable you to resist temptation as well.

The word "temptation" means "to be enticed to do evil." The enemy of our soul will always try to lead us to follow his plan for our lives or our own fleshly desires. Our fleshly nature is weak, but we can find strength because of God's Spirit in us. He can help you to stand strong in His Word the way Jesus did so that you can resist any temptation thrown in front of you.

Even though in our spirit we want to do the right thing, if we are not led by the Holy Spirit every day, we will eventually give in to our weak, sinful nature. When Jesus came to His disciples and found them asleep, He said, "Could you not watch with Me one hour? *Watch and pray, lest you enter into temptation. The spirit indeed is willing, but the flesh is weak*" (Matthew 26:40–41, emphasis added). He is saying that to us today.

The prayer that Jesus taught us says in part, "Do not lead us into temptation" (Luke 11:4), but this does not mean God is going to put temptation in our path unless we ask Him not to. It is saying that God knows where the enemy has or will set a trap of temptation for you, and you are praying that He will lead you away from that trap. It's like praying, "Lord, when You see me about to be tempted away from what You have for me, lead me away from that and in the right direction." We have no idea how important and far reaching that prayer is to our life.

God will test your love for Him by allowing certain things to come into your life that you must reject. He wants us to choose *Him* — to obey *Him,* serve *Him,* reverence *Him,* and cling to *Him* — no matter what temptation arises.

God said that if someone comes to you and says, " 'Let us go after other gods' — which you have not known — 'and let us serve them,' you shall not listen to the words of that prophet or that dreamer of dreams, for the LORD your God is testing you to know whether you love the LORD your God with all your heart and with all your soul" (Deuteronomy 13:2–3). The Bible says, "If sinners entice you, do not consent" (Proverbs 1:10). Be strong about this. Enticers are everywhere.

Resist temptation by being in the Word of God. The Bible shines a light on your soul and reveals what is in it. It gives you the strength you need to stand strong because it convinces you that God has already won the battle. This is your most powerful weapon — just as it was for Jesus. When the devil tried to tempt Jesus to do what He knew was wrong — to eat when He had been called to fast, to put God to the test by jumping off the temple to see if the angels would catch Him, and to worship Satan and gain the whole world — Jesus refuted everything the devil tempted Him to do by quoting the Word of God. We can do the same thing. We have knowledge of the Word and access to the same Holy Spirit in us.

Satan tempted Jesus by trying to undermine the sovereignty of God and His Word. Beware of someone taking one Scripture from God's Word to the exclusion of others in order to get you to do something the Holy Spirit is not leading you to do. Jesus understands how the enemy tries to tempt us away from God's best for us. "We do not have a High Priest who cannot sympathize with our weaknesses, but *was in all points tempted as we are,* yet without sin" (Hebrews 4:15, emphasis added). Because "He Himself has suffered, being tempted, He is able to aid those who are tempted" (Hebrews 2:18). Jesus helps us to resist the enemy when he tries to tempt you away from all God has for you. The Holy Spirit in you will warn you and enable you to stand strong against him.

Resist temptation with prayer. When you are faced with a strong temptation, don't think you can resist it on your own. "Let him who thinks he stands take heed lest he fall" (1 Corinthians 10:12). Always remember that "no temptation has overtaken you except such as is common to man; but God is faithful, *who will not allow you to be tempted beyond what you are able,* but with the temptation *will also make the way of escape,* that you may be able to bear it" (1 Corinthians 10:13, emphasis added).

Holy Spirit–led prayer makes a way of escape from temptation. It signals your allegiance to God and your rejection of the enemy's plans for your life.

Resist temptation by refusing to doubt God. Hezekiah was a good king of Judah who tore down the high places of idol worship. His enemy, the king of Assyria, arrogantly went to war against King Hezekiah and tried to tempt him not to trust God to save him from his attack.

But Hezekiah refused to be tempted to doubt God. Instead, he went to the prophet Isaiah for a word from the Lord. God told him, "Do not be afraid of the words which you have heard, with which the servants of the king of Assyria have blasphemed Me" (2 Kings 19:6). God promised to send a spirit upon the Assyrian king that would cause him to return home, where he would die by the sword in his own land.

The king of Assyria continued to taunt King Hezekiah, sending him a letter telling him not to let God deceive him because he was surely going to lose (2 Kings 19:10–11). Hezekiah did not respond to the threats of the Assyrian king, but instead he again took his problem to God for help. He spread the letter before the Lord and prayed. First he declared who God was and exalted Him. "You are God, You alone, of all the kingdoms of the earth. You have made heaven and earth" (2 Kings 19:15). Then he gave his request to God. "O LORD our God, I pray, save us from his hand, that all the kingdoms of the earth may know that You are the LORD God, You alone" (2 Kings 19:19).

When Hezekiah brought the threatening letter before the Lord, it was a physical act, but it was *symbolic of putting the situation in the hands of God.* We, too, can take a symbol of what frightens us, or comes against us, or tempts us to doubt God and bring it before

God in the same way. The lawsuit. The bills too large to pay. The threatening letter. The disloyal friend. The dwindling bank account statement. The sick child. The difficult spouse. The disaster. Whatever stands against us. We can bring it before God humbly in prayer and refuse the temptation to doubt God.

As a result of Hezekiah's prayer, God sent an angel to destroy the Assyrian soldiers — 185,000 of them (2 Kings 19:35). God can send whatever you need to defeat your enemy too. Don't ignore your fears, but don't wallow in them, either. Take them to the Lord and lay them at His feet. Don't listen to what evil people say. They don't know God, and they don't have the Holy Spirit of God in them. Refuse to live in the faithlessness they stir up.

Being tempted doesn't mean you are a bad person or you've done something wrong, because being tempted isn't sin. Giving in to temptation is sin.

Jesus fasted for 40 days and nights. It was at this point — doing what God led Him to do — that Jesus was confronted by Satan, who came to tempt Him away from all God had for Him. The enemy does that to us as well.

If you are doing something good for the Lord, you can plan on being tempted by the enemy of your soul to do something wrong. That's why pastors are especially targeted by the enemy. He wants them to falter and fail. And that is the reason we must pray frequently for our pastors and their families as well as for ourselves and others. The enemy wants to destroy all who spread the good news.

Anything you put above God in your life is an idol — including your wants, desires, and selfish requests. Ask God to keep you from entertaining any thoughts that give place to even the slightest suggestion of temptation. It is deadly. Let the Holy Spirit empower you to *run the other way!*

PRAYER POWER

Lord, I know You never tempt anyone, and that temptation comes only from the enemy. I pray You will make me continually aware of anything presenting itself to me as temptation. Help me to separate myself from whatever tempts me to be or do something that is in opposition to Your ways. Show me my weaknesses or sinful tendencies so that I can avoid all access to anything that feeds them. When I am tempted, help me to trust in You with all my heart and lean not on my own understanding. Help me to acknowledge You in all my ways so You can direct my paths (Proverbs 3:5–6).

Holy Spirit, lead me away from anything that presents even the most remote possibility of getting me off the path You have for me — that includes the things I see, watch, read, spend time with, or find myself becoming preoccupied by. If it is not Your best for me, I do not want it in my life. I know that "he who trusts in his own heart is a fool, but whoever walks wisely will be delivered" (Proverbs 28:26). I choose this day to trust in You and not myself. Help me to be wise and stay separate from anything that tempts me away from the high mark You have for my life.

In Jesus' name I pray.

WORD POWER

Do not enter the path of the wicked, and do not walk in the way of evil.

PROVERBS 4:14

Do not lead us into temptation, but

deliver us from the evil one. For Yours is the kingdom and the power and the glory forever.

MATTHEW 6:13

Led to Be Separate from the Past

You cannot find the wholeness God has for you if you don't separate yourself from your past. Carrying the past around with you will exhaust you to the point that you cannot go on. God has freedom from all that for you. Jesus will deliver you, and the Holy Spirit will lead you out of it and into the future God has for you.

You are not your past — you are not your father and you are not your mother — you are who God made you to be.

In order for the Holy Spirit to lead you into your own promised land — the place God has for you, where He will bless you, establish you, and make you fruitful for the work He has for you to do — your heart must be completely dependent upon Him only. That means you have to be separated from your past so that it cannot control you in any way. You don't need to have it erased from your memory, but you cannot carry it around with you, and it must not have any hold on you. You can't move into a new time carrying a load of negative old times with

180

you on your back.

Being separate from your past means you don't let it influence your life in a negative way. The main reason we let that happen is because we have not forgiven someone or some incident. Forgiving someone can be hard . . . or nearly impossible in some cases. But God forgives you of all past sins when you receive Jesus, and His Holy Spirit of love will always lead you to forgiveness and enable you to do it.

One good reason to forgive is to be forgiven. Jesus said, "Whenever you stand praying, if you have anything against anyone, forgive him, *that your Father in heaven may also forgive you your trespasses*" (Mark 11:25, emphasis added). God will not *continue* to forgive us if we don't forgive others. And we cannot live that way.

Forgiveness is the best way to separate yourself from the negative aspects of your past, and it can start immediately.

Ask the Holy Spirit to show you any places in your past where you need to forgive someone — as recently as five minutes ago or as far back as your earliest memory. Then ask the Holy Spirit to help you do that. Many times a lack of forgiveness runs so deep that forgiving someone becomes a process as God reveals layers of unforgiveness you didn't even know you had.

Another good reason to forgive is that it gives you a clear conscience before God and He answers your prayers. If you confess your unforgiveness to God, it clears the air between you. It pleases Him. "Beloved, if our heart does not condemn us, we have confidence toward God. And *whatever we ask we receive from Him,* because we keep His commandments and do those things that are pleasing in His sight" (1 John 3:21–22, emphasis added). Having clarity of mind and confidence before God, and knowing He hears and answers your prayers, are reasons enough to forgive anyone of anything.

Not forgiving won't take away your salvation, but it will take away your peace. It will hinder your intimacy with God and halt your journey into wholeness. Refusing to forgive is torturous and too much for you to bear. It takes a toll on your body as well as your mind and emotions. When you have unforgiveness toward someone, it binds you to them and keeps you in the past with them. You are never free of them or the memory of what happened until you forgive.

Forgiveness is an issue you will have to grapple with as long as there are people in the world. But the Holy Spirit will always lead you toward forgiveness. Usually, you know when you need to forgive someone, but there may be times when you don't realize you have picked unforgiveness back up again. Or there may be deeper layers you haven't gotten free of yet. Whatever the case, don't let a lack of forgiveness stop up the communication and closeness between you and God. Nothing is worth that.

PRAYER POWER

Lord, help me to separate myself completely from the past. I know You have set me free from it, and I cannot move into all You have for me if I continue to carry it with me. Deliver me from every negative aspect of it. Help me to recognize any person or circumstance from the past that I need to let go of by forgiveness on my part. Help me to be so separate from my past that it doesn't negatively influence the present or keep me from moving into the future You have for me. Help me to forgive so that I can be forgiven (Luke 6:37). I don't want the torture of not forgiving to destroy my mind, body, and soul (Matthew 18:34–35). I know that forgiving someone doesn't make that person right, but it *will* make me free.

Reveal to me any specific person or incident I still have resentment toward so I can confess it as sin and be set free of it. Enable me to let it go completely so that nothing stands in the way of my moving into all You have for me. Help me to forgive others the way You have forgiven me — completely and unconditionally (Ephesians 4:32). I want to always do what is pleasing in Your sight. Lead me, Holy Spirit, into the light of forgiveness, so that I am not stumbling in the dark (1 John 2:10–11).

In Jesus' name I pray.

WORD POWER

Forget the former things; do not dwell on the past.

ISAIAH 43:18 NIV

Be kind to one another, tenderhearted, forgiving one another, even as God in Christ forgave you.

EPHESIANS 4:32

Led to Be Separate from All Pride

The Holy Spirit will always lead you away from pride. The enemy of your soul will inevitably try to draw you into it. The enemy, who is pride personified, will come to you with his lies and tell you that you are great and highly deserving, that you don't have to live by the rules, and that you alone are responsible for whatever you accomplish and the good things that happen to you.

If you ever find yourself entertaining these kinds of thoughts, *RUN, DON'T WALK,* in the other direction. The enemy is trying to take you down, and if you don't get away from his influence, he will.

God does not tolerate pride. He says it is rebellion, like witchcraft. The Bible says, "In the last days perilous times will come: For men will be *lovers of themselves, lovers of money, boasters, proud, blasphemers, disobedient to parents, unthankful, unholy*" (2 Timothy 3:1–2, emphasis added). Each of these things has pride as its root.

Whenever you experience any kind of blessing or success, the enemy will try to tempt you with pride, so be prepared to reject it.

A good example in the Bible of not following the leading of the Lord, but instead being led by pride and greed for material pos-

185

sessions, is a man named Gehazi. He saw that the prophet Elisha had refused to take payment from a man called Naaman, who offered the payment to Elisha for helping him be healed of leprosy. So Gehazi lied to Naaman, saying that Elisha badly needed what Naaman had offered to give him. Naaman then gave that payment to Gehazi. But instead of Gehazi giving the payment to Elisha as he said he would, he hid it away in his own house (2 Kings 5:1–24).

When Gehazi saw Elisha again, he lied to Elisha about where he had been, even though the Lord had revealed the truth to Elisha about what had happened. Elisha declared that now Naaman's leprosy would come upon Gehazi's body instead, and it would be with his descendants forever (2 Kings 5:25–27).

There are extremely serious consequences for giving in to pride, greed, and lying to God instead of following the leading of the Holy Spirit.

Uzziah began as a good king in Judah because he did what was right in the sight of God. "*As long as he sought the LORD,* God made him *prosper*" (2 Chronicles 26:5, emphasis added). However, he became full of pride over all the good things he had done instead of giving credit to God. "*His heart was lifted up,* to his destruction, for he transgressed against the LORD" (2 Chronicles 26:16, emphasis added). In his pride he disobeyed God and then became a leper and "was cut off from the house of the LORD" (2 Chronicles 26:21).

That is not a small thing.

The fall that is preceded by pride is always an enormous one. It will ruin your life. If you truly understand that God has given you everything you have, you will never be prideful about it — especially if you are not fond of lightning striking at very close range.

No matter how faithful you think you are, anyone can succumb to pride. Even though you are not a prideful person, an evil spirit of pride can put prideful thoughts in your mind. It can happen before you know it. I have seen it happen to people whom I never thought it would. Refuse to think that the good things happening to you are all because of you. Give God glory for every blessing and success you have.

After all that God had done for King Hezekiah, in his success he still became prideful. God had given Hezekiah so much that he "prospered in all his works" (2 Chronicles 32:30). But at a certain point, "God withdrew from him, in order to test him, that

He might know all that was in his heart" (2 Chronicles 32:31).

When Hezekiah was visited by the son of the king of Babylon, who came on a goodwill visit, he proudly showed the prince everything he had. When the prophet Isaiah asked Hezekiah what he had shown the Babylonians, Hezekiah said, "They have seen all that is in my house; there is nothing among my treasures that I have not shown them" (2 Kings 20:15). Because of Hezekiah's pride in showing off his possessions instead of humbly recognizing that all had come from God, Isaiah prophesied that everything he had would be carried off to Babylon. And that was precisely what happened.

The pride that nearly destroyed Hezekiah can destroy us too. We are all susceptible to it. Its consequences are devastating, so ask the Holy Spirit to show you even the slightest beginning of pride in your heart. If any is revealed, humbly ask Him to take it away. It is never worth the consequences that are sure to come.

Pride is a huge issue. When God gives you success, separate yourself from all pride. Don't even allow yourself a moment of it. If you find yourself thinking heady thoughts, such as *I must be really good at what I do or I wouldn't be so successful,* or *I don't need to seek God in this particular area because I know what I'm doing,* or *I deserve this no matter what I have to do to get it,* or *I'm better than those people,* ask God to cleanse your heart. If you become prideful, God may allow failure to happen to you in order to prove without a doubt that you are not as great as you thought you were.

Ask the Holy Spirit to cause flashing red lights and screaming sirens to go off in your brain if you don't recognize pride in your heart. Pride is a great destroyer. It is the trait that caused Satan to fall from heaven. Don't you fall for that too.

PRAYER POWER

Lord, I thank You for everything You have done in my life, and I praise You for each blessing You have given me. I know that all good things come from You, and I am forever grateful for them. Forgive me if I ever attempt to take credit for what I have or accomplish instead of giving glory to You. Keep me from entertaining pride in my heart. Show me if prideful thoughts begin to take hold in my mind. I know that pride

189

is opposed to all that You are, and it is rebellion against You if I take credit for what You alone have done.

Show me prideful thoughts immediately when they enter my mind. Give me the ability to recognize the enemy's tactics and refuse his lies. I know that pride will bring me down, but humility will keep me honorable (Proverbs 29:23). I don't want to do anything that keeps Your Spirit from manifesting Himself fully in my life. I want to have a humble heart at all times (Proverbs 21:2). Establish my heart "blameless in holiness" before You (1 Thessalonians 3:13). I know that "a good man out of the good treasure of his heart brings forth good things" (Matthew 12:35). Fill my heart afresh with the treasure of Your Holy Spirit and lead me away from pride that is the root of all evil.

In Jesus' name I pray.

WORD POWER

All that is in the world — the lust of the flesh, the lust of the eyes, and the pride of life — is not of the Father but is of the world.

1 JOHN 2:16

Pride goes before destruction, and a haughty spirit before a fall.

PROVERBS 16:18

Led to Be Separate from All That Draws You Away from God

God wants the fire of His presence to never be allowed to grow cold. That fire keeps burning as long as you are in communication with Him, but it can cool when outside influences draw you away from spending quality time with Him.

God wants you to separate yourself from anything that separates you from Him and all He has for you.

God told His people, "Circumcise the foreskin of your heart, and be stiff-necked no longer" (Deuteronomy 10:16). For us that means He wants us to cut away anything from our heart that makes it distant from Him. God requires that we reverence Him, live His way, love and serve Him with all our heart, and keep His commandments (Deuteronomy 10:12–13). Whatever interferes with any of that in our lives must be eliminated.

Of course sin separates us from God, but there are more subtle things that can do that as well, such as busyness; obsessing over our work to the exclusion of all else; or allowing other people, the Internet, or television to occupy all of our time. Ask the Lord to show you where things in your life are competing with Him for your attention.

Below are just a few of the countless things we must be rid of, because they swallow up our valuable time and draw us away from the intimate walk with God that He wants us to have.

Get rid of any influence that compromises your relationship with God. The Israelites did not obey God by completely driving out the Canaanites in the Promised Land as God had commanded them to do (Joshua 15:63). Instead, they allowed them to stay as slaves (Joshua 17:12–13). But by remaining in their midst, the Canaanites planted seeds of dissension among them. What we must learn from this is to separate ourselves from all that God tells us to drive out of our lives.

Allowing anything or anyone to stay in your life that is not of the Lord will compromise your relationship with Him and draw you away from His best for you. You have to be separate from the noise of your life in order to hear what the Holy Spirit is speaking to your heart. Ask the Holy Spirit to reveal anything like that to you.

■ ■ ■ ■

Get rid of jealousy or covetousness. Whenever you want something of someone else's,
it is an example of having an idol in your
heart. Coveting someone else's possessions,
spouse, success, business, ministry, talent,
abilities, or relationships wastes your time.
Admiring what someone has is different than
coveting what they have and desiring to have
it for yourself. Seeing what someone has
and being happy for them is different than
seeing it and feeling envy. There is a fine
line that happens in the heart, and we can
cross that line without even realizing it.

Ask the Holy Spirit to reveal anything in
your heart or mind of a jealous or envious
nature from which you need to be free. Being jealous is depleting and leads to self-
pity, which goes against all that God has for
you. It will always draw you away from
God's best because it is a sign that you are
not grateful for what He has already given
you or will give you in the future.

Get rid of striving to be like other people. We
get into trouble trying to emulate someone
or some lifestyle that is not of the Lord
because of an overwhelming desire to fit in.

When we want to be admired by people more than we want to please God, it takes our heart, focus, and time away from Him.

The Israelites wanted a king. God told Samuel that having a king would mean that the ruler would take many of their sons, daughters, crops, and possessions, and they would cry out to God because of it. But the people *wanted to be like all the other nations* (1 Samuel 8:10–20). Because they wanted to be like ungodly people, they suffered the loss of so many of the blessings God had for them.

When you spend time trying to be like someone else, it takes time away from becoming all God created you to be.

Get rid of any tendency to be controlled by money. We can gravitate toward securing money or possessions to the exclusion of being fully committed to God. These things are not wrong to have if God gives them to us for His purposes, but if not, striving for them can separate us from all God has for us.

A rich man wanted to know what he could *do* to inherit eternal life because he had obeyed all the commandments (Mark 10:17–20). Jesus said, "One thing you lack: Go your way, sell whatever you have and give to the poor, and you will have treasure in heaven; and come, take up the cross, and follow Me" (Mark 10:21). The rich man was sad about this because "he had great possessions" (Mark 10:22). Wealth had become an idol to him.

Jesus didn't say that all wealth is bad. God does not say we cannot have material things. All through the Bible He blessed His loved ones with wealth and material things. But He does not want material things to control us. They can never become more important to us than following God. It's amazing how money — the quest to get it and the things we can do with it — will draw us away from the things of God if we let it.

Ask the Holy Spirit to reveal to you anything in your life that draws you away from the Lord. He will begin to open your eyes to whatever wastes your valuable time and energy for no earthly benefit.

PRAYER POWER
Lord, help me to separate myself from anything that draws me away from You. I don't want to waste valuable time and effort on things that have no value for my life. Reveal to me any way I have done that or am doing it now. Help me

to recognize all unworthy distractions that compromise who You have called me to be and all You have for me to do. Enable me to eliminate everything in my life that keeps me from serving You in the way I should. Give me the ability to see as worthless the things *You* see as worthless too.

I don't want to in any way put a damper on my relationship with You by allowing things into my life that water down my commitment. I pray that my desires are so submitted to You that they never cause me to violate Your best for my life. I so very much need to be refreshed and strengthened by the times I spend with You that I don't want any unnecessary distractions to keep me from receiving all that. Help me to establish right priorities. Enable me to remember who You made me to be so that I don't violate that by reaching for something to fill me when I should be filled by only You.

In Jesus' name I pray.

WORD POWER

Draw near to God and He will draw near to you. Cleanse your hands, you sinners; and purify your hearts, you double-minded.

JAMES 4:8

Let us draw near with a true heart in full assurance of faith, having our hearts sprinkled from an evil conscience and our bodies washed with pure water.

HEBREWS 10:22

6
Led to Be Transformed

One of the great purposes of the Holy Spirit in us is to transform us into the image and likeness of Christ. The Holy Spirit will always lead us toward becoming more like Him every day.

The truth is you become like what you behold. "We all, with unveiled face, beholding as in a mirror the glory of the Lord, *are being transformed into the same image* from glory to glory, just as by the Spirit of the Lord" (2 Corinthians 3:18, emphasis added). The more you look to the Lord, the more you will become like Him.

Our concept of God affects who we are and what we become. Our view of God determines how we view our life and how we behave. Some of the problems we have may be brought on because we have an anemic idea of who God is. Or we've never had *any* idea about who He is. Our soul is always affected by the way we see God and what we think of Him.

We can see where this is absolutely true when we look at our own life. Or the lives of others. It's easy to observe the lack of fruit in the lives of those who have a lowly concept of God. By contrast, those who have a highly exalted and reverential view of God are fruitful. The greater your idea of God, the deeper your walk with Him will be.

When you invite the Holy Spirit of God to work in you, you cannot keep your own transformation from happening.

God knows you and sees your potential.
A. He knows you the way you are right now.
B. He knows who He made you to be.
C. He knows how to get you from A to B.

We can say to God as King David did, "You have searched me and known me. You know my sitting down and my rising up; You understand my thought afar off. You comprehend my path and my lying down, and are acquainted with all my ways. For there is not a word on my tongue, but behold, O LORD, You know it altogether" (Psalm 139:1–4).

God knows everything about you. How great is that?

God knows where you are. He also knows where you are *supposed* to be. And He knows how to get you there. You can never go so far away from Him that you no longer have His Spirit in you. "Where can I go from Your Spirit? Or where can I flee from Your presence? If I ascend into heaven, You are there; if I make my bed in hell, behold, You are there" (Psalm 139:7–8).

Doesn't that knowledge give you greater confidence to face life?

God knows your future. You are not an accident. It doesn't matter who your parents were or what they did; you were not a surprise to God. And your future is planned. "You formed my inward parts; You covered me in my mother's womb. I will praise You, for I am fearfully and wonderfully made; marvelous are Your works, and that my soul knows very well . . . in Your book they all were written, the days fashioned for me, when as yet there were none of them" (Psalm 139:13–14,16). If the future God has for you is written in God's book already, then the only one who can keep it from happening is you.

Doesn't that make you feel that God cares about you and you're not just wandering alone through life?

God thinks about you all the time. He has a personal interest in your life, and His thoughts are always toward you. "How precious also are Your thoughts to me, O God! How great is the sum of them! If I should count them, they would be more in number than the sand; when I awake, I am still with You" (Psalm 139:17–18). Proof that He is always with you is His Holy Spirit in you.

Does God think about you more than you think about *Him?*

Jesus said that the kingdom of heaven is like a mustard seed — the smallest of seeds — and it grows into something big (Matthew 13:31–32). It is also like leaven that spreads and penetrates people's lives in a transforming way (Matthew 13:33). That's the way God's kingdom penetrates your life. By the power of the Holy Spirit in you, it grows and affects every part of you — including your mind, emotions, and character. The Holy Spirit will always lead you toward transformation. *God's plan is to bring you to complete wholeness by the power of His Spirit in you.*

Led to Be Transformed in Your Mind

Being transformed starts when you make a decision to receive Jesus and be filled with God's Holy Spirit. That decision you made with your mind affects your entire being. We are instructed, "Do not be conformed to this world, but *be transformed by the renewing of your mind,* that you may prove what *is* that good and acceptable and perfect will of God" (Romans 12:2, emphasis added).

To "be transformed" means to completely change form. And that's what the Holy Spirit of God enables us to do as we submit to Him. The more we walk with God and invite His Spirit to be in us in fullness, the more our thought life is changed.

We are regenerated when we receive Jesus and His Holy Spirit is given to us, but transformation takes time as we walk with Him and are led by His Spirit.

To be transformed also means to *keep on being transformed.* It is a metamorphosis from the inside out. We are transformed in some way every time we are in the Lord's presence. The more we spend time with the Lord, the more we become like Him.

When you come to the knowledge of the truth in Jesus, it is important "that you *put off, concerning your former conduct,* the old man which grows corrupt according to the deceitful lusts, and *be renewed in the spirit of your mind,* and that you *put on the new man* which was created according to God, in true righteousness and holiness" (Ephesians 4:22–24, emphasis added). That means we are to stop doing things the way we used to — giving place to lust, disobedience, and rebellion — and we are to be renewed in the spirit of our mind so that we can put on the new self God has given us and live right.

We have to live in distinct contrast to what is going on in the culture of the world around us. We are to not walk in the futility the rest of the world walks in, having no understanding about life, living in a manner that is alienated from the ways of God, and having a heart that is blinded to the truth and a mind that is ignorant, or ignoring, of God's ways. Don't let the world make you conform to its way of thinking when you can be transformed to God's.

Your mind affects you more than you think. It can keep you in darkness even when you have the light. It can keep you in old habits and patterns of thought and far from all God has for you. It is with your mind that you reason, understand, and make decisions. It is in your mind when you decide to be good or evil. When your mind is controlled by the Holy Spirit, you have peace, contentment, and rest.

Being spiritually minded is good. Being carnally minded is bad. "Those who live according to the flesh set their minds on the things of the flesh, but *those who live according to the Spirit, the things of the Spirit. For to be carnally minded* is death, but *to be spiritually minded is life and peace*" (Romans 8:5–6, emphasis added). Our carnal mind will always be at odds with God. We are setting ourselves up as an enemy of God if our carnal mind controls us. That's because our carnal mind is not subject to God's laws.

We must make a decision every day to turn away from evil and the flesh, and seek to live directed by the Holy Spirit.

If we live in the flesh, we cannot please God (Romans 8:8).

We don't want to be people "whose minds the god of this age has blinded, who do not believe" (2 Corinthians 4:4). We don't want to be like those who "resist the truth" and have "corrupt minds" (2 Timothy 3:8). We want to be people whose thoughts please the Lord.

The following is true about your mind.

You have the mind of Christ. "Who has known the mind of the LORD that he may instruct Him? But we have the mind of Christ" (1 Corinthians 2:16, emphasis added). That means you always have access to right thinking. You can correct your thoughts whenever you get off course by turning to the Lord and thanking Him that you have the mind of Christ. Don't let the enemy of your soul tell you any different.

You are able to love God with your entire mind. Jesus said, "You shall love the LORD your God with all your heart, with all your soul, and *with all your mind*" (Matthew 22:37, emphasis added). When we make a decision to love God with everything that is in us, that choice crowds all that is not of the Lord out of our mind.

Your mind can be implanted with God's laws. God said, "I will put My laws in their mind and write them on their hearts; and I will be their God, and they shall be My people" (Hebrews 8:10). When you read or speak God's Word, God can etch His laws in your mind so you do not forget them. You may not remember every exact word, but you know what the laws are. Ask Him to help you recall them with clarity anytime you want to.

Your mind can be free from corrupting and futile thoughts. Paul said, *"Your minds may be corrupted from the simplicity that is in Christ"* (2 Corinthians 11:3, emphasis added). He also said, "You should no longer walk as the rest of the Gentiles walk, in the futility of their mind" (Ephesians 4:17). The world makes things complicated. Jesus simplifies everything for us if we choose to follow Him. Our thoughts become futile when they are not brought under the Lordship of Jesus.

Your mind is made sound by the Lord. God has given you "a sound mind" (2 Timothy 1:7). If you don't think you have a sound mind, you can ask Him for it. We all know when our mind feels unstable, tormented, or crazy, and we don't have to put up with it. Having a sound mind leads to wholeness in our entire being. The Holy Spirit will always lead you to possess the sound mind God has given you.

206

■ ■ ■ ■

The change ignited in your spirit when you open up to the love of God affects your mind. The negative things that used to occupy your thoughts no longer have the appeal they once did. When you experience the mind of Christ, you no longer want anything less. While there will still be battles in your mind between your old self and your new self, don't be discouraged by that. Your old habits of thought that keep trying to control your life will disappear as the Holy Spirit continuously renews your mind.

Just as our body is the temple of the Holy Spirit and we can choose to treat it badly, our mind is the Lord's and we can fill it with junk. We have a sinful nature, and our natural mind is at odds with God. But our mind can be radically changed when we submit our thoughts to Him. Sin can make our mind clouded and distracted so that it is unclear or confused. When our mind is cleansed from all that by the Lord, we must make a specific effort to fill it with the things of God.

Studies on the effect that people's thoughts and emotions have on their body show that negative, wrong, and evil thoughts affect physical health more than they may realize. Your mind affects your body. If your thoughts can make you sick, then they can also make you well. Don't ever forget that.

PRAYER POWER

Lord, I pray You will renew and transform my mind. Help me to think clearly. Give me the ability to reason solidly. Enable me to secure a steady mind-set on everything I face and every situation I am in. I know that the transformation of my mind will mean the transformation of my entire life, including my health. I know You always see what is in my mind (Jeremiah 20:12). Show me anything in my mind that is not of You. Help me to bring every thought captive in obedience to You (2 Corinthians 10:5). Teach me to dwell on things that are true, noble, right, pure, lovely, admirable, excellent, or praiseworthy (Philippians 4:8 NIV). Help me to refuse any thoughts to the contrary.

Enable me to identify any lies of the enemy I am accepting as truth. I know a big part of standing against the enemy of my soul is to take control of my mind. I know that You, Holy Spirit, cannot lead me into all You have for me if I listen to the enemy telling me lies about myself or my circumstances. I pray that the mind of Christ in me will crowd out anything that is not of You. May Your peace, which is beyond all understanding, guard my heart and mind through Christ Jesus (Philippians 4:7).

In Jesus' name I pray.

WORD POWER

God has not given us a spirit of fear, but of power and of love and of a sound mind.

2 TIMOTHY 1:7

Casting down arguments and every high thing that exalts itself against the knowledge of God, bringing every thought into captivity to the obedience of Christ.

2 CORINTHIANS 10:5

Led to Be Transformed in Your Emotions

Emotions are the intense feelings we have in response to what *is* happening, or what *has* happened, or what we feel *might* happen. Our emotions are affected by the thoughts we think in our mind. Our thoughts produce the emotions. If the thought is negative, it produces a negative emotion. If it is positive, it produces a positive emotion. God created us with the ability to feel emotions. We are made in God's image, so that means He also feels sadness, anger, and grief. Feelings are good if the thought inspiring them is right.

The following is true about your emotions.

God cares about people who are emotionally broken. "The LORD is near to those who have a broken heart" (Psalm 34:18). In His presence our hearts are made whole and our emotions become positive.

We can guard and control our emotions. "Keep your heart with all diligence, for out of it spring the issues of life" (Proverbs 4:23). We can change our emotions with the truth of God's Word. God speaking to your heart from His Word can take away negative emotions.

Emotions can crush us. "A merry heart makes a cheerful countenance, but by sorrow of the heart the spirit is broken" (Proverbs 15:13). A broken spirit happens when the level of sadness in your life becomes unbearable.

Positive emotions are their own reward. "He

who is of a merry heart has a continual feast" (Proverbs 15:15). When we are inundated with negative emotions, they bring destruction within ourselves. But we have a choice as to whether we will entertain them.

The emotions of anxiety and depression can be changed with the right words. "Anxiety in the heart of man causes depression, but a good word makes it glad" (Proverbs 12:25). Encouraging words bring greater healing of negative emotions than we even imagine. A word from God to your heart is even better than what any person can say.

The Holy Spirit in you is a deposit God puts in your soul that means you are tied forever to Him and will be drawn to Him when you die. That knowledge alone can take away the dark clouds and release light into your heart.
We often feel that our emotions are just the way we are and we cannot change them. But when our emotions are subject to the control of the Holy Spirit, we can get free of the negative ones. The Holy Spirit will always lead us away from negative emotions. That doesn't mean we deny our feelings. Pretending we don't have them doesn't solve the problem; it makes it worse. God gave us the ability to feel things. God sees

everything — including what we are feeling. Because He is God and His Holy Spirit is in us, "there is no creature hidden from His sight, but all things are naked and open to the eyes of Him to whom we must give account" (Hebrews 4:13). He knows what is in your heart. He knows what you are going through in your emotions. Where there have been deep wounds, He wants to heal them.

God wants you to bring your emotions and feelings to Him. Acknowledge before Him when you are sad, lonely, anxious, or hopeless. He has a remedy for all of that. He wants to give you His joy in place of sadness. When you feel lonely, He wants to give you a sense of *His* love for you. When you are anxious, He will give you His peace. When you feel hopeless, He will be your hope. He has a cure for every painful, negative, or tormenting emotion you may have. His cure is to deliver you from them completely so that you can become the whole person He created you to be.

We all love the familiar and distrust the unfamiliar. The unfamiliar, or the unknown, can be frightening. There are many people who will stay in a negative situation because it is familiar, rather than go where there is a promise of something good, because that would be unfamiliar. We have to get to the point where we become so familiar with the presence of God's Spirit that anything less feels foreign. We must walk so closely with the Lord that we feel most comfortable in His presence and uncomfortable when we are not.

PRAYER POWER

Lord, I thank You that I don't have to live with negative emotions that do nothing good for my mind, soul, and body. Show me where I am living with sadness, anxiety, fear, loneliness, bitterness, unforgiveness, or any other negative attitude. Break any control these emotions have on me. Replace them with the fullness of Your Spirit of love, peace, and joy. I pray that You will crowd out everything in me that is not of You. You know the secrets of my heart (Psalm 44:21). Show them to me when I can't see them myself, and renew a right spirit within me.

I pray for a transformation in my heart so that I can step out of old habits of feelings and emotions that are paralyzing and limiting my life. "Search me, O God, and know my heart; try me, and know my anxieties; and see if there is any wicked way in me, and lead me in ie way everlasting" (Psalm 139:23–24). Help me to "be anxious for nothing, but in everything by prayer and supplication, with thanksgiving," I will make my requests to You so that Your peace, "which surpasses all understanding," will guard my heart and mind through Christ Jesus (Philippians 4:6–7). I pray my spirit will be so filled with Your joy that it sustains me in sickness (Proverbs 18:14) and becomes medicine to my body (Proverbs 17:22).

In Jesus' name I pray.

WORD POWER

Those who wait on the LORD shall renew their strength; they shall mount up with wings like eagles, they shall run and not be weary, they shall walk and not faint.

ISAIAH 40:31

The LORD is near to those who have a broken heart, and saves such as have a contrite spirit.

PSALM 34:18

Led to Be Transformed in Your Character

Your character is who you really are all the time, whether you are alone and no one is watching, or you are with peers who put pressure on you to be a certain way, or you are in a group of people, whether godly or not.

Character has to do with morals, principles, values, integrity, honesty, attitude, decency, virtue, honor, faithfulness, loyalty, trustworthiness, respectability, morality, responsibility, and a sense of right and wrong. Each of these words can be broken down to get an even finer description of what goes into having good character. Good character is who you are on the inside and how that shows up on the outside.

We know who we want to be, but we are powerless to permanently change who we are without the power of the Holy Spirit in us enabling us to do so.

When you receive Jesus and are filled with the Holy Spirit, you have the source of your transformation within you. That's because the Holy Spirit will always lead you away from "business as usual." You stop doing things the way you used to. When you are renewed in the spirit of your mind, your emotions are renewed and you can put on the new self God has given you. Your very character is transformed.

Your new self chooses to live in distinct contrast to everything that is opposed to the Lord. You no longer choose to walk in the futility the rest of the world walks in, having no understanding about life, living in a manner that is not of the Lord, and being alienated from His purpose for your life. You no longer have a mind that is ignorant of God's truth, nor a heart that chooses to be oblivious to it. You become kind, tender-hearted, and forgiving because you know that "God in Christ forgave you" (Ephesians 4:32). You have greater confidence about the future because you know that the Holy Spirit dwells in you and you are the Lord's forever. You become aware of what grieves His Spirit, so you refuse to do anything that will cause Him to be grieved.

Transformation of your character means going from being selfish to being selfless, from living in the dark to living in the light. But not everyone experiences that. We've all seen Christian people who go to church but have character defects that never seem to change. They display loveless attitudes or continue on a path of wrongdoing. Why does their character not seem to improve? It could be because they have refused to acknowledge the Holy Spirit. Or, if they do acknowledge Him, He is relegated to a place where He can neither manifest Himself in their lives nor touch them in any way. They do not allow the Holy Spirit to empower them to rise above themselves and make choices that reveal "righteousness, faith, love, and peace" which is formed in their character when they "call on the Lord out of a pure heart" (2 Timothy 2:22).

As you give place to the flow of the Holy Spirit, He will form in you new character that looks more and more like the character of Christ.

God told the Israelites, "Be holy; for I am holy" (Leviticus 11:44). Peter explained it further, saying that "as obedient children, not conforming yourselves to the former lusts, as in your ignorance; but as He who called you is holy, you also be holy in all your conduct" (1 Peter 1:14–15).

That sounds easy, right?

No, it sounds impossible. How can we do that? Not on our own, that's for certain. Jesus said, "You shall be perfect, just as your Father in heaven is perfect" (Matthew 5:48). That's impossible too, isn't it? Yes, it is when we try to do it on our own.

We often think that holiness is not attainable and so we avoid the subject. But holiness is like wholeness. The Holy Spirit works in us to make us holy and whole. Being holy is not some vague and invisible concept we never really know if we have attained and always doubt that we have. The Holy Spirit has released us to "be partakers of the divine nature" (2 Peter 1:4). But we must cooperate with Him in every way in order to see that happen.

If the Lord is working in you until the day you go to be with Him, then it seems holiness is a process of becoming more like Jesus every day. The brokenness in your heart, emotions, and spirit can be mended, and those broken pieces can be brought together to make you a whole and holy person. Now *that's* transformation.

PRAYER POWER

Father God, help me to be an imitator of You as one of Your children. Teach me to walk in love, as Christ also has loved me and gave Himself for me as an offering and a sacrifice to You as a "sweet-smelling aroma" (Ephesians 5:1–2). Enable me to imitate You in all I do. Help me to walk as a child of light, even in the dark places (Ephesians 5:8). "For You are my lamp, O LORD;" You "shall enlighten my darkness" (2 Samuel

22:29). Form good character in me.

Teach me to reject all works or acts of darkness immediately, not even tolerating them around me. I don't want to even glance at the things evil people say or do, for I know that "it is shameful even to speak of those things which are done by them in secret" (Ephesians 5:12). Enable me to always walk in the Spirit and not in the flesh. Thank You, Jesus, for saving me, delivering me, and freeing me. Change me to be more like You. Make me holy, as You are holy. Thank You, Holy Spirit, for leading me. It is only by Your power that I can be freed from the pull of my flesh to do what it wants and released to live the life of holiness You have for me. I know that transformation is found in Your presence.

In Jesus' name I pray.

WORD POWER

We also glory in tribulations, knowing that tribulation produces perseverance; and perseverance, character; and character, hope.

ROMANS 5:3–4

Not by works of righteousness which we have done, but according to His mercy He saved us, through the washing of regeneration and renewing of the Holy Spirit.

TITUS 3:5

7
LED TO SEE PURPOSE

When you have given your life to the Lord and surrendered to the leading of God's Spirit in you, one of the things the Holy Spirit will reveal is what God has purposed for your life. First, He will help you to understand that you are not some random accident, no matter what the circumstances were surrounding your birth. God didn't say, "Oops" when you were born. Your arrival may have surprised your parents, but it didn't surprise God. He had a plan for your life when you were conceived, and you have a purpose.

The unfolding of that plan doesn't just happen haphazardly or randomly either. In fact, the discovery and fulfillment of your purpose happens only as you seek God and follow the specific directions of His Spirit. Day by day, little by little, God will reveal it.

When Jesus asked Peter, "Who do you say

that I am?" Peter answered and said, "You are the Christ, the Son of the living God" (Matthew 16:15–16). Jesus then said to him, *"Flesh and blood has not revealed this to you, but My Father who is in heaven"* (Matthew 16:17, emphasis added). Paul said of the gospel, "I neither received it from man, nor was I taught it, but it *came through the revelation of Jesus Christ"* (Galatians 1:12, emphasis added).

It is through revelation from God that you acknowledge Jesus as Messiah, and it is through revelation from God by which you receive understanding of what God wants to do in you and through you.

You cannot fulfill your purpose — meaning *God's* purpose for you — without being totally submitted to Him and willing to follow His leading in every aspect of your life. You must become fed up with trying to live life your *own* way, or the *world's* way, or the way of the *enemy,* and instead have a strong desire to live *God's* way. Only as you are living God's way can you even begin to *see* your purpose. And only as the Holy Spirit leads you can you head in the right direction, stay on the path God has for you, and fulfill God's plan for your life.

Without the leading of the Holy Spirit, you don't know for certain if you are exactly where you're supposed to be.

Led to See Purpose in Your Reason for Getting Up Every Day

Let's start with the basics. We must have a reason to get up every day, otherwise there will come a day when we won't want to. Without a clear reason to live we can become sick, discouraged, depressed, or hopeless. We will want to hide, run away from home, tell everyone to get out of our life, or, worse yet, do something destructive to ourselves. And if the work you are doing or the activities you are engaging in are not God's will for your life, you will have a deep frustration within you that will build continually until you cannot take another step. And you won't know what to do about it if you don't have revelation from God. Without the Holy Spirit leading you, you can waste your life.

The Bible says God's mercies are new every morning (Lamentations 3:22–23). Don't you love that? The mercy He has shown you in the past does not dissipate, run out, or grow weak. He has *new* mercies for each day. Because of His mercies, every day of your life can be a new beginning. Who doesn't need that?

Today may not feel like a new beginning

to you. It may appear to be the "same old, same old." This is especially true if you have been beaten down by circumstances, or you have suffered loss, or you have been chained to your past, or you have had to endure abusive people in your life who tear you down rather than build you up, or if you are around self-righteous people who view you with the face of a judge and the heart of a hostile jury looking for evidence to prove you guilty. You will have a harder time hearing the voice of God's Spirit to your soul above the condemnation of the enemy. You can become so depressed and discouraged from all that *is* happening, or *has* happened, or you fear *won't* happen in your life that you can barely function. But the good news is that God has total freedom from all of this for you.

You can get up every morning with hope in your heart, knowing God has everything you need to rise above the challenges of each day and to move into all He has for you.

Each morning when you wake up, you have a choice as to whom or what you will follow. There is the possibility every day that, in a moment of weakness, you will choose the wrong path — the way of the flesh and not the Spirit, the way of the enemy and not the Lord. When you decide the moment you get up to follow God, His Spirit will always lead you away from living in the flesh.

The Holy Spirit will never lead us to be angry or impatient with others, nor immoral, self-indulgent, rude, or cruel. If we are that way, it is because we have not made the *choice* to crucify our flesh and submit to the leading of the Holy Spirit that day. It's because we have not gotten up that morning and said, "Thank You, God, for this day. Thank You, Jesus, for saving me and setting me free. Thank You, Holy Spirit, for leading me in everything I do. Thank You, Lord, that there is nothing impossible with You." In fact, write those words on a card and put it where you will see it every morning and say them to the Lord when you wake up. Make them a habit.

While the Holy Spirit reveals your purpose in life and enables you to accomplish God's will, you still have to choose to follow His leading every day.

God is there for you each morning — not to mention midmorning, noontime, afternoon, high tea, dinnertime, early evening, midnight watch, and in the middle of the night. There is never a time when God is not reaching out to you with His love, waiting for you to reach out to Him. His compassion never fails (Lamentations 3:22). He always has a heart for you.

So much of the trouble and heartbreak we experience is because we don't have a sense of God's purpose in our life and we don't follow the leading of the Holy Spirit. God doesn't want you to barely survive. He wants you to know that you have a reason to live and a great purpose in doing so.

Too much of the world in your life can dilute your understanding of who God is and what He has planned for you. That's why it is so important to fill your mind with the Word of God early in the day before everything else that is vying for your attention starts to crowd in. Establish *who* you are *with,* and *who* is *with* you. And trust God's Holy Spirit directing your steps toward the fulfillment of the very reason you are here — *to be with Him, to serve Him, and to fulfill your purpose.*

PRAYER POWER

Lord, help me to be filled with a sense of Your love, joy, peace, and purpose every morning when I get up. Enable me to know with all certainty that You are with me and I am not alone. Strengthen my faith to understand without doubt that You, Holy Spirit, will guide me every step of my way. I submit to You everything I face today and ask You to help me successfully walk through it with strong faith that can move mountains. I believe nothing is impossible with You, Lord, and because of that there is no mountain that is insurmountable.

Help me to see Your purpose for my life. I know that without that sense of purpose I can end up making wrong choices and fall into the enemy's trap. I know my sense of purpose in life will keep me on the correct path and headed in the right direction. Where my vision for Your purpose in my life has become blurred, give me clarity. Even if I don't know all the details, I know *You* do. And I trust You to lead me always toward the fulfillment of that purpose. My soul waits on You, Lord, more than those who watch for the morning (Psalm 130:5–6). Keep me always aware of where it is You are *not* taking me so that I will avoid making time-wasting mistakes. Thank You, Lord, that You "will perfect that which concerns me" (Psalm 138:8).

In Jesus' name I pray.

A man's gift makes room for him, and brings him before great men.

PROVERBS 18:16

Awake, you who sleep, arise from the dead, and Christ will give you light.

EPHESIANS 5:14

Led to See Purpose in the Gifts God Has Put in You

When you have the Lord breathing new life in you each day, you will come to understand that your life has purpose — not because others say so, which doesn't hurt, but because *God* says so. He views you in light of the high purpose He has for you.

No matter what has happened in your past, God has placed gifts within you that are to be used for His glory.

By depending on God each day, and trusting in His Word, and learning to follow the leading of His Holy Spirit, you will be able to discern the gifts and talents God has placed in you. Perhaps all you have in the beginning is a strong desire to do a particular thing, or something you enjoy doing, or an ability to do something that comes naturally, or a skill you have learned. The way to recognize your gifts is to ask God to show you what they are. Don't discount anything. An ability you have may not strike you as important, yet God can use it for His glory in a powerful way.

Some people have obvious gifts and talents at an early age, but that doesn't mean they will choose to use them for God's glory. We see people with great gifts using them for the enemy's glory all the time. Some people cannot see their gifts early on at all, but that doesn't mean they aren't there. Many people may not discover their gifts until later in life — gifts they never dreamed they had.

Everyone has gifts and talents. No one is without them. You are no exception.

Some people have the ability to do many things, and that can be a problem for them because it is hard for them to choose which one to focus on. That's why they need to hear from God. He may use them all. He can open or shut doors of opportunity according to His purposes.

Many people think they don't have any gifts, often because their parents, or perhaps someone else significant in their life, didn't ask God to reveal their gifts so they could be developed and nurtured. If that has happened to you, don't let it concern you. It doesn't matter if your gifts weren't revealed to you early on. The Holy Spirit can reveal them to you now — today — or in the days to come.

If you are one who believes you don't have any special gifts, know that God often works most powerfully through a person who depends totally on Him for the manifestation of any gifts He has given him or her. Don't wait to feel qualified. God wants to use you to do things you *know* you can't do without *Him.* He will use your gifts powerfully when you rely on Him.

Don't rely on your own abilities, or you will find yourself limited by them instead of being empowered by the Holy Spirit.

While it's true that we all have gifts, those gifts will not bear the fruit God wants them to without our submission to the Holy Spirit. He is our Helper who enables us do what God calls us to do. We all have abilities we are born with, and we need to identify and nurture those gifts and talents and develop them to be used for the Lord. Ask the Holy Spirit to lead you in the discovery and recognition of your gifts. Even if you have been moving in your gifts for years, ask Him again. The Holy Spirit may want to redefine the gifts He has put in you — not to change them necessarily — in order to prepare you for a new level of their use and a new time in your life. He is always refining and preparing you for what is ahead.

There are other gifts — spiritual gifts — given to us by the Holy Spirit as we walk with God and are to be used for His purposes. "There are diversities of gifts, but the same Spirit" (1 Corinthians 12:4). The Holy Spirit does not force spiritual gifts upon us. He releases them *in* us for the benefit of others. He says these are gifts we should desire, but we must remember that they are *His* gifts and not ours.

These spiritual gifts are not to be confused with our natural God-given gifts God uses in our lives for His purpose. Spiritual gifts are spiritually discerned, and the Holy Spirit gives them to us as He wills. We cannot manipulate them or force them. You don't have to worry that if you surrender yourself to the Lord, He is going to force a spiritual gift on you. It won't happen. The Holy Spirit does as *He* wills, but not against *your* will.

We are given spiritual gifts in order to help others and not for our own glory. This is extremely important to understand. The Bible says, "The manifestation of the Spirit is given to each one for the profit of all: for to one is given the *word of wisdom* through the Spirit, to another the *word of knowledge* through the same Spirit, to another *faith* by the same Spirit, to another *gifts of healings* by the same Spirit, to another the *working of miracles,* to another *prophecy,* to another *discerning of spirits,* to another *different kinds of tongues,* to another the *interpretation of tongues.* But one and the same Spirit works all these things, *distributing to each one individually as He wills*" (1 Corinthians 12:7–11, emphasis added).

I am not going to discuss the individual gifts in this book. There are countless opinions on this subject, and I don't want to list the opinions of men about the Word of God. I am telling you what God's Word says on the subject, and you are perfectly capable of hearing from God as the Holy Spirit teaches you about Himself. Ask Him to show you the truth and "He will teach you all things" (John 14:26).

God chooses what gift each one receives. It is not according to our natural abilities. It's not according to what we have done to deserve them, because we can never do anything to *deserve* the gifts of the Spirit. We don't claim the gifts. God gives us spiritual gifts according to what His will is and what His purposes are.

While we can't decide what spiritual gifts we have, we can do things to inhibit the flow of these gifts of the Spirit in us.

Don't worry about whether you have a spiritual gift or you don't. Paul says to desire them (1 Corinthians 12:31), but let the Holy Spirit give them as He wills. That means there is no reason to be prideful if God gives you a gift. And there is no reason to be ashamed, feel inferior, or be disappointed if you are not given one. This is entirely the Holy Spirit's operation, not ours. Desire the gifts, but don't worry about them. Be open to them, but don't covet another's gifts.

Personally, I have moved in two of the gifts a number of times. One is the word of knowledge and the other the gift of faith. They have happened at different times and always when I was in prayer — either alone or praying with someone. In these instances it was entirely the Lord. It had nothing to do with what I was "thinking about" or had "been feeling" or anything like that. And it was beyond what I could do on my own. And I knew without a doubt at the time that the gift was from God.

In one instance, for example, I was in prayer for my pastor and his wife and family. And I heard God speak to my heart these words, *"Satan wants to pierce Pastor Jack's heart."* I knew that was clearly a word from the Lord. So I asked God to tell me more.

"Lord, how does the enemy plan to do that? In what way?"

The Lord impressed clearly upon my heart, *"Through one of his grandchildren."*

When I asked which one, the Lord gave me a clear picture of a specific granddaughter.

I didn't call the pastor and tell him right away because I thought perhaps this was revealed to me just so *I* would pray about it. But God didn't allow me to have peace about it until I finally made the call. I had never called Pastor Jack before with a word of knowledge, so he didn't take it lightly. He called his entire family to meet that afternoon, and they prayed together about this.

Not long after this happened, Pastor Jack and his son-in-law, Scott, were cleaning his garage when the littlest granddaughter got out of the house and ran to find her dad and grandpa. The large and heavy two-car garage door spring was broken, and the door was being propped open by a pole. They were ready to leave the garage and go in the house for dinner when Scott knocked the pole out of place, and the heavy garage door came slamming down just as the little girl came running around the corner. Her dad yelled, "No!" and Pastor Jack reached out his hand from where he was standing and stopped it just before it hit her head. She would have been crushed by it. As tears filled their eyes, Pastor Jack said, "That was it. That was the warning from the Lord to pray." One second later and she could have been killed or severely injured.

When I found out what had happened, I thanked God for the word I knew was from Him. I have had that experience with a word of knowledge a number of times, and I always take it seriously and never hold back from telling the person whom it is regarding.

The other gift is the gift of faith. I have strong faith, and I believe the Word of God and the Lord's promises to us and what He can and wants to do in our lives. But the spiritual gift of faith is way beyond that. It is a gift God gives us for that time and for a specific person or situation. I cannot conjure this up. It has nothing to do with me and everything to do with God. I *wish* I had that kind of faith all the time. It is strong, clear, powerful, and unwavering, and there is no doubt whatsoever with it. A gift of the Spirit is not something you wonder if that's what it is. You *know* that's what it is.

Each time I have had a gift of faith, it seems to come not only from *within* me, but also it comes *upon* me like a mantle put over my head and shoulders that covers me. And it becomes the way I feel led to pray. It's as if God is saying, *"This is what you are to pray, and I am giving you the faith to believe for it as if it has already come to pass."* I know without doubt this is the voice of God to my heart, and by praying about it as the Holy Spirit leads me, it is settled in the spirit realm before it manifests itself in the physical realm.

The Bible says to desire the gifts and I do. But I don't claim or demand the gifts. They are from the Holy Spirit and are there when it is God's will for the benefit of someone else. In the gift of faith I was always praying for someone about a specific need, and I felt led to pray a certain way. And God gave me faith so strong that it was as if the prayer had already been answered.

In one particular situation like that, I was praying for a young woman to have a child. She and her husband had been trying for years, but they had finally given up and were now trying to adopt, and she asked me to pray that they would be given a baby soon. As I was praying for that request — which I enjoy doing because I think adoption is one of the most beautiful and touching manifestations of God's love — I was given the gift of faith to pray that she would conceive. This was not my idea. I didn't have a desire either way. I had nothing at stake in this. But I had a gift of faith that led me to pray for their biological child as well. And what happened was they were given a child to adopt within that year, and not long after that she delivered their biological child as well.

The spiritual gifts God gives are quite diverse, but each person doesn't get them all. God knows we could not control our pride if that were to happen. They come from the Holy Spirit in us. That's how we receive what God wants us to have. This "manifestation of the Spirit" that Paul talks about is given to us for the betterment of everyone. They have nothing to do with our natural ability. They are given by the Holy Spirit for a specific purpose, and they cannot be obtained any other way.

God works through the spiritual gifts He gives people. We have to learn how to receive them, open up to them, embrace them, use them, and grow in them.

PRAYER POWER

Lord, I pray that You would reveal to me the gifts and talents You have put in me. Enable me to understand their value to You. Where the gifts I want don't line up with the gifts I have, help me to submit those desires to You and allow You to be in control. Develop the gifts You have put in me so that they become useful for Your kingdom. Teach me to move in excellence with them, always knowing that I have not perfected them, but it is *You* who have done it. I pray that any insecurity in me — which I know is actually a lack of faith in Your ability to guide and sustain me — will not rule over my using the gifts You have placed in me.

Lord, Your Word says that I am predestined according to Your purpose for my life (Ephesians 1:11). But I know I cannot fulfill that destiny without following the leading of Your Holy Spirit day by day in my life. I desire Your spiritual gifts in obedience to Your Word (1 Corinthians 14:1). Use me for Your purposes as You see fit. Help me to stay closely connected to You by the power of Your Spirit in me so that I will always follow Your leading. In all I do, help me to never lose sight of Your high purpose for my life.

In Jesus' name I pray.

WORD POWER

May He grant you according to your heart's desire, and fulfill all your purpose.

PSALM 20:4

My beloved brethren, be steadfast, immovable, always abounding in the work of the Lord, knowing that your labor is not in vain in the Lord.

1 CORINTHIANS 15:58

Led to See Purpose in God's Call on Your Life

God has a call on your life. And He gives you the gifts you need in order to equip you to fulfill that calling. These gifts help you do what God calls you to do, and He doesn't take them back (Romans 11:29).

People are not called because they are wise, talented, powerful, or prominent (1 Corinthians 1:26). They are called according to God's purposes for their lives. We are "predestined to be conformed to the image of His Son" and *"whom He predestined, these He also called;* whom He called, these He also justified; and whom He justified, these He also glorified" (Romans 8:29–30, emphasis added).

In order to fulfill your purpose in life — without which you will never know the fulfillment God has for you — you must not only seek God and follow the leading of His Spirit, but you must also understand how God wants you to use your gifts to serve Him and what He is calling you to do. He wants you to "be even more diligent to make your call and election sure, for if you do these things you will never stumble" (2 Peter 1:10).

Sometimes people hear the call of God on their lives before they even know what their gifts are. When God calls you to something that you don't "feel prepared for," you can trust that God will equip you to do it. Your gifts will become apparent as you step out in faith. So if you feel you don't have what it takes to fulfill your calling, then rejoice, because you are going to have to depend on God for everything you need. And although it may seem scary to you at the moment, it is actually the best position to be in, because it has to be all *Him* or it's not going to happen.

It is possible to exercise your gifts without giving any heed to your calling. Too many people do that. That's how they can use their gifts in ministry and still cheat on their wife or be unfaithful to their husband. If you are married, preserving that marriage is the biggest part of your ministry and calling. If you are not called to be married, don't be married. But don't get married and then decide you are not called to be married. Or say, "I am called to be married, only just not to this person I'm married to right now." If God has given you the gift of children, they are not something you can take back or exchange for something else. You are called to take care of them. Your gift will not lead you to abandon your marriage or your children. If you feel led to do that, go before the Lord, confess that, and find out what your calling *really* is.

When God calls you, He will equip you as well. An Angel of the Lord appeared to Gideon and told him, "Go in this might of yours, and you shall save Israel" (Judges 6:14). So Gideon said to Him, "O my Lord, how can I save Israel? Indeed *my clan is the weakest* in Manasseh, and *I am the least* in my father's house" (Judges 6:15, emphasis added). And the Lord gave Gideon the reason he could do this, saying, "Surely *I will be with you*" (Judges 6:16, emphasis added). *The Lord equips you with His presence* to do what He calls you to do.

When the disciples received power as the Holy Spirit came upon them, they became witnesses to Jesus wherever they went (Acts 1:8). God wants to do the same with you. He wants His Holy Spirit to work *in* you in order to work *through* you to reach others with His love and the truth. He does not reside in each of us to do *our* bidding so that *we* can have a happy life. He works in us to help us become more like Jesus so that we can live the life *God* has called us to live.

When we are led by the Holy Spirit, our transformed life becomes a witness to the power of God as the Holy Spirit enables us to speak about Jesus and the things of God to others.

When God calls you, He will refine you. God gave a song to Moses to teach to the Israelites that would warn them of the consequences of their corruptness, foolishness, and lack of wisdom. The song gives a picture of God hovering over us and carrying us as an eagle hovers over her young and carries them on her wings (Deuteronomy 32:11). This is the way the Lord wants to lead us today. He will take us to heights we cannot imagine, but *we have to stay as close to Him as possible,* or we will fall and not be able to get where He wants us to go.

When we walk close to the Lord, He *refines* us. Fire is a symbol of the Holy Spirit. Only the refining fire of the Holy Spirit burns away what is not good or needed. It doesn't damage or hurt us, but if we are not purified, the enemy can put a hook in us that can be our downfall. The Bible says, "Do not quench the Spirit" (1 Thessalonians 5:19). The word "quench" means to put out or extinguish, to subdue or destroy a fire. We don't want to put out or destroy the fire of the Holy Spirit in us. We will stifle all that He wants to do through us when we don't welcome Him to use us for His glory.

God wants to empower you to be used mightily, but if you try to accomplish that apart from the refining fire of the Holy Spirit that comes to ready you, you are destined to fail.

The only way we can be an effective instrument of God's love, peace, and power is to be purified by the Holy Spirit in us and by our obedience to the Word of God.

When God calls you, He gives you peace about it. Without the leading of God's Spirit, we cannot know anything about what is to come. How can we look far into the future when we don't know what will happen tomorrow? The only way we can move successfully into our future is by walking step-by-step with God today, following the leading of the Holy Spirit in whatever we are doing now. The future is unknowable apart from any revelation God may give us. And even with revelation from the Lord, we don't know all the details about it. We just know that God says we have a good future, and this gives us peace.

When God calls you, He will put a dream in your heart of what needs to be accomplished. When God puts a dream in your heart and gives you a vision for the future, He doesn't want you to try to realize that dream or fulfill that vision in your own strength. He wants you to surrender to Him completely, and then He will bless you with an anointing of His Spirit and a new release of His presence and power in you. God will equip you for what He has for you to do. But you must seek Him for it.

If the dream you have in your heart does not in any way match the call God has on your life, surrender your dream to the Lord. It if is not of Him, He will take it away and replace it with His.

When God calls you, the Holy Spirit will enable you to do what you need to accomplish. We are not all just dangling out in space trying to serve a demanding God. Not in the least. God has high expectations of us, but He wants us to depend on Him to see those expectations realized. When we submit to Him, choose to live His way, and listen for the leading of His Spirit in our lives, He will enable us to accomplish and fulfill those expectations.

God wants us to have high expectations of Him too. What He gives us to do is always far more than we can accomplish on our own, and He will make certain we are convinced of that. He will bring us to a place in our lives where we recognize that there is no way on earth we can do it without Him, but we can expect that with God, all things are possible. And because of that, He can enable us to fulfill our calling.

Just as a pregnant woman says, "I'm expecting," you can say you are expecting God to birth something great in you.

When God calls you, the enemy will try to thwart what God has called you to do. God's enemy and your enemy is one and the same. Satan's name means "adversary." Jesus called him the evil one (John 17:15). He has hostility toward all believers and will always come to discourage you from what God has called you to. He will try to *trouble* you and stir up someone to resist your work. That's why it is important to always know clearly what God has called you to do and what He has *not* called you to do. Intimidation and fear are two of the enemy's tactics. The enemy says, "You cannot do it." But *you* know that through Christ you can, because He who has called you is also able to make it happen.

Always confront the lies of the enemy with the truth of God's Word. Trust the leading of the Holy Spirit in your heart more than the voice of your enemy threatening you. Be careful to always live consistently with what God has called you to do.

PRAYER POWER
Lord, open my eyes to see what I need to see about Your calling on my life.

Open my ears to hear Your voice leading me into it. Prepare and equip me for what You have for me to do. Keep me from doing anything that would violate or compromise that. I know that much will be required of me, and I ask that You will help me to fulfill those requirements. I cannot do what You want me to do without the power of Your Holy Spirit enabling me to do it. Refine me to become a pure vessel through whom You can work. Help me to submit to that refining process.

Teach me to always be able to identify the ploys of the enemy trying to discourage me with his lies. Help me to never fall for his deception so that I don't get off the path You have for me. Keep me from doing anything that would hinder all You want to do in and through me. I pray that You, the God of my Lord Jesus Christ, the Father of glory, will give me the spirit of wisdom and revelation so that my eyes of understanding will be enlightened and I will always know what is the hope of Your calling on my life (Ephesians 1:17–18).

In Jesus' name I pray.

The gifts and the calling of God are irrevocable.

ROMANS 11:29

I, therefore, the prisoner of the Lord, beseech you to walk worthy of the calling with which you were called.

EPHESIANS 4:1

8
LED TO BEAR GOOD FRUIT

When you have the Holy Spirit in you, and you daily seek His leading, you will find yourself becoming more creative and productive in every area of your life. That's because you are tapped into the ultimate creative force — our God, who created the universe and all things in it.

Where God's Spirit is, there is creativity and fruitfulness.

If you immerse yourself in the Lord and keep yourself from the pollution of the world, His voice in you will become clearer. He will guide you, inspire you, and reveal to you things you would not have seen on your own. When you submit your own natural creative ability to the Lord, *His* creativity will flow in you and your life will bear fruit.

The Holy Spirit gives us spiritual fruit, but the degree it grows in our lives is up to us. The Bible says, "The fruit of the Spirit is *love, joy, peace, longsuffering, kindness, goodness, faithfulness, gentleness, self-control*" (Galatians 5:22–23, emphasis added). When these virtues become visible in you, this is a good sign the Holy Spirit is working powerfully in your life.

The first three fruit of the Spirit are feelings and attitudes that are like God. They are the *love* of God, the *joy* of God, and the *peace* of God that passes all understanding. These are who God *is*. He *is* love. He *is* peace. He *is* joy. And He gives to us all that *He is* through His Holy Spirit in us. If you find you don't have enough love, joy, or peace in your heart, get closer to God by spending time with Him in His Word, in prayer, and in worship. Remember, He pours Himself into you when you worship Him.

The second three fruit of the Spirit are the way we should be, especially around other people, animals, and God's creation. They are *patience* (which is longsuffering), *kindness,* and *goodness.* We need the patience of Job. Patience to wait on God. Patience with people and situations that try our patience. We need kindness. The consistent type of kindness that never fails and is no respecter of persons. Kind to all at all times. We need goodness. The goodness of God.

That's the kind of goodness that manifests itself even when people don't deserve it. *God* is good *all* the time, no matter how bad *we* are. But we can't be good all the time without *His* goodness being produced in us.

The third group of the fruit of the Spirit has to do with the way we act. They are *faithfulness, gentleness,* and *self-control.* Each one is beyond our own natural tendency to perfectly express. Unless the Holy Spirit produces such spiritual fruit in us to the degree that God wants, we will always be lacking in these areas. We cannot grit our teeth and make ourselves always have self-control, for example, but the Holy Spirit can produce self-control in us all the time.

When the Holy Spirit controls our life, He produces these nine virtues in us. But too often we choke off His work with negative emotions, such as fear, anger, sadness, doubt, impatience, unforgiveness, and judgmentalism — the opposite of the fruit of the Spirit. We can even allow someone else's rudeness to hinder the spiritual fruit crop growing in us.

Being filled with the Spirit changes our character, but we still have to *choose* to live in the Spirit. "Those who are Christ's have crucified the flesh with its passions and desires. If we *live in the Spirit,* let us also *walk in the Spirit*" (Galatians 5:24–25, emphasis added). When we walk in the Spirit, the fruit of the Holy Spirit will manifest itself in us in amazing ways.

Led to Bear Good Fruit in Your Life

In order to produce good fruit in our lives, we have to plant the right seeds. Even the smallest seed we plant can grow into something big. And we can begin to see good fruit right away.

Jesus said, "I am the vine, you are the branches. He who abides in Me, and I in him, bears much fruit; for *without Me you can do nothing*" (John 15:5, emphasis added). We cannot bear good fruit without Him.

In order to produce good fruit in your life, not only do you have to plant good seeds, but you must also pull up and cast out the *bad* seeds. That means your personal habits must be submitted to the Lord so that they glorify Him. I know this is a tough one, because your personal habits are . . . well, personal. And we often think our private habits are our own. And they are, as long as they don't interfere with God's purpose and plan for your life.

Jesus also said that He is "the true vine," and His Father God is "the vinedresser," and every branch in Him *that does not bear fruit* He takes away; and *every branch that bears fruit He prunes, that it may bear more fruit*" (John 15:1–2, emphasis added). We are the branches that cannot bear fruit without being connected to the True Vine. But we must be pruned by the Vinedresser.

If you are not producing good fruit, perhaps you have not given the Holy Spirit full access to your life. Or maybe it is a just a timing thing. Perhaps you are not seeing the *full* crop of good fruit *yet.* Maybe more pruning is needed. Maybe just more time is needed.

When we lived in California, I was able to grow the most beautiful rosebushes. I had about 40 bushes in many stunning colors. They produced roses so profusely in the spring and summer that people would drive by just to look at them. I carefully picked some every day to put in a vase in the house or to give to someone. I fed and watered them diligently.

I dreaded when the petals inevitably started to fall off the roses and it was time to prune them back. We had a man come to do that because the thorns were brutal and he knew how to do it right. But after he did it, the poor bushes looked like a bunch of naked sticks — pathetic bare dead wood, nothing to admire. And it seemed as though they were that way for the longest time; at least, until spring came around again and the green leaves sprouted and the buds began to appear.

Seasons in our lives are like that. We may have been producing fruit and then suddenly it feels as if that fruit has been cut off and we are left like a dead stick. We may think we must have done something wrong to lose the favor of God. But this is a time of pruning, *getting rid of all that is not necessary in our lives in order to produce new fruit.* It is a time of deep inner growth. It may not be evident to someone else that this is going on, but we can feel it.

Pruning is a necessary work of the Holy Spirit that eventually frees us to bear more fruit in the future. Even though it may feel as if the life we knew is over and there is no future, God is actually preparing us for a new harvest.

If that happens to you, it can make you feel as though you have been put out to pasture and God doesn't want to use you or your gifts anymore. But take heart. Unless you are walking in sin, this is when God is preparing you for a new season of fruit-bearing. People sometimes give up during this period, believing God has forsaken them or given up on *them.* But that is far from true. Cling to the Lord and refuse to entertain any doubt about what God is doing in your life. Trust Him with all your heart. Go deeper with Him. Read the Bible more. Pray more. Pray with other believers. Find people you can help in some way. That won't be hard; they are everywhere. Be God's hand extended to others.

Even though pruning is uncomfortable, we should welcome it. The Holy Spirit will strip away from us certain attitudes, habits of thought and action, unnecessary possessions, and goals that are not what the Lord wants for us now. He will change the ways we have always done things, not because they were bad, but because He wants to do a new thing.

God doesn't strip away anything we can't live without, even though it may feel like it at the time. Our flesh may resist, but in our spirit we can even feel relieved, because God wants us to simplify our lives so that we can better do what He has called us to do. We can say, "Lord, what do I have in my life that should no longer be there?" Letting go of unnecessary things frees us to receive more of what God wants to impart to us.

We are commanded to bear good fruit. And when we do, we will draw others to Jesus. Only good fruit that comes from the Holy Spirit in us is lasting. We've all seen people who do not bear good fruit. They cannot produce the fruit of a good spirit because they don't have a good spirit in them. Even if they are a believer, the Holy Spirit cannot function to His fullest in someone who ignores or denies the Holy Spirit in them.

Jesus said, "Beware of false prophets, who come to you in sheep's clothing, but inwardly they are ravenous wolves. *You will know them by their fruits*" (Matthew 7:15–16, emphasis added). That's because a "good tree bears good fruit, but a bad tree bears bad fruit" (Matthew 7:17). He said that "every tree that does not bear good fruit is cut down" (Matthew 7:19).

Any sin without repentance will keep someone from bearing good fruit. The fruit of the Spirit will be visible only in a person who lives in obedience to God's ways.

When our flesh is in control, we do things we don't want to do. It is a constant battle. I have seen the good fruit of someone's ministry change once the flesh of that person gained control away from the Spirit. He may even have even been unaware of it in the beginning, but he didn't stop what he was doing in time to cast out the bad seeds and turn it around. Pride made him think he could get away with disobedience.

Pride makes people believe they are entitled to do *what* they want, *when* they want. It's a work of the flesh that blinds our eyes. It is what causes people who know better to do wrong. It happens all because the flesh was allowed to gain control instead of the Spirit being consistently *invited* to be in control. It can happen to any one of us in a weak and unmonitored moment. If you see pride in yourself, humble yourself before the Lord and confess it. If you see pride in someone else, RUN! There is about to be a great fall, and you don't want to go down with them. Pray for that person to have their eyes opened to the truth.

The more the Spirit of God has free access in your life and the more room He is given to grow in you, the more you will exhibit the fruit of His Spirit.

We don't have to strive to produce good fruit in our lives. We just have to stop planting bad seeds and learn to plant only the good ones. We must walk daily with Jesus, remain in Him by following the leading of the Holy Spirit in us, stay in constant communication with Him, and more and more surrender our lives to His control. This is not something we *make* happen. It is something we choose to *let* happen.

However, fruit cannot grow apart from the light. We are children of the light who are filled with the fruit of the Spirit, which "is in all goodness, righteousness, and truth" (Ephesians 5:9). We are not to have anything to do "with the unfruitful works of darkness" but instead "expose them" (Ephesians 5:11). We all walked in the dark before we received Jesus, but now, as children of the light, we must get rid of anything that blocks His light in us and keeps us from bearing spiritual fruit. When we exhibit the fruit of the Spirit, God is glorified, and it is a sign that we are His disciples (John 15:8).

PRAYER POWER

Lord, I pray You will help me to bear good fruit in my life. Teach me how to plant the right seeds in my heart. Grow up what has already been planted in me from Your Word. I know that every moment I spend in Your presence in worship, praise, and prayer waters, nurtures, and grows the seeds of Your character in me. Keep me from doing anything to inhibit that process. Grow a crop in the good ground of my heart that produces a hundredfold (Matthew 13:8). Search my heart and show me any bad seeds that have been planted there so that I can uproot them and cast them out. I submit myself to Your pruning process. Help me to let go of anything in my heart or my life that should not be there. Keep me from all pride. I don't want anything to prevent me from bearing the fruit of Your Spirit in my life.

I pray that people will sense Your love, joy, and peace in me, and they will be attracted to You because of it. I pray that the fruit of Your Spirit will manifest itself in me so powerfully that others cannot help but notice it and glorify You. Enable me to exhibit patience, kindness, and goodness to others. Help me to have Your faithfulness, gentleness, and self-control so that I can reflect the nature of Christ in everything I do.

In Jesus' name I pray.

He shall be like a tree planted by the rivers of water, that brings forth its fruit in its season, whose leaf also shall not wither; and whatever he does shall prosper.

PSALM 1:3

Either make the tree good and its fruit good, or else make the tree bad and its fruit bad; for a tree is known by its fruit.

MATTHEW 12:33

Led to Bear Good Fruit in Your Work

There's one thing you will always see in a believer's life who follows hard after God and is led by His Spirit, and that is fruit in their work. The truth is, you can't fight fruit. In other words, you can't deny it when you see it. I'm not saying there aren't difficult times of struggle. We all go through that. Times of growth, learning, and pruning can all be painful, but there is fruit on the other side.

If you are *not* led by the Holy Spirit in the work you do, you will not bear the good fruit God wants you to produce. If you are not empowered by the Holy Spirit, you are not producing fruit for eternity the way God desires. Your work and ministry has to be modeled after that of Jesus, who was empowered by the Holy Spirit and did nothing that wasn't directed by His Father God.

Whatever your work is, submit it to the Lord. Ask Him to infuse it with His life, power, and productivity. Ask Him to flow His Spirit through you and enable you to be more creative. When you do that, it's possible you may even be led out of the work you are doing at present and into something else if what you are doing is not what the Lord wants.

We don't tell God what we are going to do and ask Him to bless it. Instead, we ask Him what He wants us to do, and do what He says so He can bless it.

In a grocery store, fruit is called "produce." That's because when the right seeds are planted, watered, and fed, fruit is produced. Can you assess the productivity of your life — maybe not in the past, but in the time since you have closely followed the Lord? Has your influence or affect on others been positive and good? Has it helped people? Do they see and experience something of the Lord because of you? If you are letting God lead you by the power of His Holy Spirit, you will see Him bless what you do.

I knew a man who was contentious, judgmental, explosive, and selfish to the point of hurting others. The weeds of his flesh suffocated the growth of his creativity. When he hindered the work of the Holy Spirit in him with sin, it stopped God's blessings on his work. The good news is when that happens, it can be turned around by a repentant heart. It was a long time coming, but that is what eventually happened with this man. Repentance bears fruit. Always! God can bring dead things to life when we repent. Repentance leads the way to spiritual growth and creativity. It is way undervalued in some circles.

Don't set your expectations too low with regard to what God will produce in you and through you. It will be far more than you can imagine. And don't let your expectations of yourself be so high that you cannot appreciate the fruit He is producing in your life right now. Put your expectations in the Lord. Expect that He will keep His Word and produce great things in and through you.

If you feel you are not bearing fruit in your work or ministry, ask the Lord to show you any place where you have not obeyed Him. God blesses the work of an obedient child of His (Deuteronomy 12:28). Find out what is good and acceptable to the Lord and do it (Ephesians 5:10). Fast and pray. Seek a fresh infilling of His Spirit. When you are filled with and led by the Holy Spirit, you will produce fruit in your work.

The Holy Spirit will equip you for the work He has for you to do. When the temple was being built, God asked for gifted artisans to come and make what He commanded them to make. God filled one of the artists with the Holy Spirit and gave him "wisdom and understanding, in knowledge and all manner of workmanship, to design artistic works" (Exodus 35:31–32). The Holy Spirit equipped this man to do what God was calling him to do. The Holy Spirit also "put in his heart the ability to teach" (Exodus 35:34). God not only equipped him to do the work, but He also enabled him to teach others how to do it as well.

The Bible says of the artisans that God "filled them with skill to do all manner of work" (Exodus 35:35). In other words, *the Holy Spirit enabled their giftedness.* They obviously had some abilities, but the Holy Spirit enabled them to skillfully do exactly what God wanted them to.

What the Spirit calls you to do, He will also enable you to accomplish. If He leads you to do something you don't want to do or believe you cannot do, ask Him to work a change of heart in you. I know that is scary, but He is not going to ask you to do something that is not ultimately His best for your life.

Find God's purpose in all the work you do. After Moses and the people had finished all the work, labor, and sacrifice for the building of the tabernacle, "then the cloud covered the tabernacle of meeting, and *the glory of the LORD filled the tabernacle*" (Exodus 40:34, emphasis added). The ultimate purpose of what we do for the Lord — our obedience to what He instructs us to do — is to have the presence of God with us. That says it all. All of their time, work, and sacrifice was rewarded by the greatest gift possible — the Lord's presence. In that moment it all makes sense. In that moment you don't ask, "Why, Lord?"

God gave Moses the laws of how the sacrifices were to be made, and to us they may seem impossibly strict. They go on and on, and if we lose sight of the purpose of them, they become tedious and hard. *But the entire purpose for these laws was to have a holy people so that the presence of God could visit them.* When the glory of the Lord appeared to the people and "all the people saw it, they shouted and fell on their faces" (Leviticus 9:23–24). At that moment, what they had been doing for God became clear.

You may not be able to see right now what the purpose is in all that you are doing in your work. Sometimes your work may be tedious and you lose sight of the reason you are doing it, but if you are following the Holy Spirit, it will one day become very clear. That's when you sense the magnificent presence of God's Spirit manifesting itself through you in a way that you have not seen before. You want to sacrifice whatever is necessary in order to make room for a greater fullness of God's presence in your life.

PRAYER POWER

Lord, I pray You would help me to bear fruit in my work and ministry. Help me to glean everything I need from Your Word. Teach me to plant good seeds in prayer and worship. Empower me to bear the kind of fruit that lasts for eternity. Keep me from setting my expectations too low with regard to all You want to do through my work for You. Help me not to set them so high that I don't appreciate what You are doing in me every day. Enable me to always do what *You* want. I want to be able to claim the gift of Your presence in my life as my greatest reward.

Teach me how to examine my own work and see if it meets Your standards (Galatians 6:4–5). Give me new and creative ideas so that I never get in a rut and slow down production, for I know that my creativity comes from You as a source that never runs out. Help me to do all my work with the right attitude because I am doing it for You. Enable me to do it well so I can excel in all You call me to do. Help me to see You, Jesus, as my role model. I know You never did anything that wasn't empowered by the Holy Spirit. I want to live that way too.

In Jesus' name I pray.

WORD POWER

A good man out of the good treasure of his heart brings forth good things, and an evil man out of the evil treasure brings forth evil things.

MATTHEW 12:35

They shall still bear fruit in old age; they

shall be fresh and flourishing.

PSALM 92:14

Led to Bear Good Fruit in Your Relationships

Fruitful relationships are not the kind where two people are attached at the hip and are so codependent that one can't function without the other. They are not the kind where one demands too much from the other and there is a constant drain on the relationship. A fruitful relationship does not have one person controlling the other, or always making the other person sad or fearful. Fruitful relationships are those that allow each other to be who God made them to be.

In a fruitful relationship, the fruit produced by that relationship is . . . wait for it . . . good! That is your criteria. When you are always being insulted, hurt, ignored, demeaned, or made to feel bad about yourself, the relationship is not producing good fruit. If the relationship is not worth the expense of time and money to work things out, then move on to relationships that are positive. Get out of it, if at all possible. If your difficult and unfruitful relationship is your marriage, obtain some kind of counseling together. It doesn't glorify God for either of you to be miserable in it.

It is crucial to bear good fruit in your relationships. You cannot carry on a relationship that takes you away from God, leads you to do wrong things, or causes you to have to shrink down from who God made you to be. The best seeds to plant in any relationship are seeds of prayer, love, compassion, and giving of yourself. In fact, the good fruit of any relationship comes from giving on both parts.

When we don't give in our relationships, we stop up the blessings God has for us in them, and we cannot produce a harvest of His fruit.

You may be saying to yourself, "Isn't it always good to give?" The answer is yes . . . and no. It is always good to give *when you are led by the Lord.* But if you give to someone without the Lord's leading, you can do a disservice to that person. We are to help people, but we are not supposed to try and be God to them. If you are constantly bailing out someone whom God wants to teach to trust Him, then your giving is not producing good fruit. You are creating a dependency on *you* and *not* on *God.* There is a fine line between the two, and only the Spirit of the Lord will help you to discern that.

Pride is one of the biggest obstacles to

bearing good fruit in a relationship. When we have pride we "become conceited, provoking one another, envying one another" (Galatians 5:26). Provoking another person happens when we are unkind and do things that are abrasive. When we are led by the Spirit, we will extinguish pride and exhibit every one of the fruit of the Spirit.

Your compassion for people who struggle with fear, addiction, low self-worth, physical limitations, or other challenges will become your passion to help them when led by the Spirit. The productiveness of your life will increase amazingly when it is fueled by a Holy Spirit–ignited love for other people.

The Bible says we cannot move on together in a relationship unless we are in unity with that person. We have to be in agreement with what is right, moral, and decent. We have to agree on who God is and how we relate to Him. If you don't agree on those things, then one of you will have to bend to the other. The relationship will have limited fruitfulness until there is a positive change.

PRAYER POWER
Lord, I pray You will show me which relationships to cultivate and which to let go of if necessary. Where there is one

or more that are not of You and will never produce good fruit, I pray You will reveal that to me so I can remove myself from them. I know we must have unity of spirit and like-minded in our beliefs. I pray for honesty and uprightness in all of my relationships so they can produce the good fruit You want them to. Send into my life godly relationships that will always bring glory to You. Heal all strife in any relationship I have now and make it fruitful. If it can't be made good, show me so that I can end it.

Lord, I thank You for Your work in my life. Help me always to walk with the leading of Your Spirit and to choose not to walk in my flesh. Fill me afresh with Your Spirit every day and take away any sin or selfishness from my heart. Take away all pride, criticism, envy, unkindness, or lack of love in me, or in anyone with whom I have a relationship. Show me how to give of myself to others in a compassionate yet balanced way. I don't want to try to be You to people. I want to be myself with people and allow them to be who they are too. Lead me, Holy Spirit, to do the right thing in every relationship I have.

In Jesus' name I pray.

Two are better than one, because they have a good reward for their labor. For if they fall, one will lift up his companion. But woe to him who is alone when he falls, for he has no one to help him up.

ECCLESIASTES 4:9–10

Can two walk together, unless they are agreed?

AMOS 3:3

9
LED TO DISCERN

The Holy Spirit will always lead you toward greater discernment in your life. Discernment actually has to do with seeing the truth from God's perspective. The more you are led by the Holy Spirit, the more discerning you will become. He will show you things you couldn't see before. You will have greater certainty about God's voice speaking to your heart. God will communicate with you in ways that may surprise you.

Moving into this kind of spiritual discernment doesn't happen automatically. You have to seek God first in all things and be in His Word searching for the truth. Anyone can read the Bible, but only those whose eyes have been opened by the Holy Spirit can begin to see the truth in all its fullness. And as you do, you will not only see the truth about your own life and circumstances, but you will observe the world around you with new eyes as well.

In the maze of deception and confusing information that is out in the world, you will need discernment from God in order to successfully navigate through it.

Scripture tells us that King Asa "became diseased in his feet, and his malady was severe; *yet in his disease he did not seek the LORD,* but the physicians" (2 Chronicles 16:12, emphasis added). Asa refused to ask the Lord for discernment about his disease. The physicians whom he sought may have operated by sorcery and magic, which ours don't do today. (Or, at least, let's pray we never end up with a doctor who does.) How many times do we take medicine or see a doctor without praying about it first? This is not in any way to say that we shouldn't seek medical help. But we should always seek God first before we do anything. Ask Him to heal you, and then ask if you should see a doctor or go to a hospital. Pray for the doctors you see to have great knowledge, wisdom, and discernment.

Because Asa did not seek the Lord for discernment about that, there were serious consequences for him. The point is that there are serious consequences for us as well when we don't seek God first in all things and then make decisions without the discernment He could have given us.

The Holy Spirit in you can reveal whatever you need to know at any given moment, but you must seek Him for it.

The Holy Spirit is your guide. But if you never acknowledge Him as that, or you deny Him that position in your life, you restrict His ability to guide you. He will never barge in and break down a wall to force you to follow Him. He is not a control freak. A control freak takes over whether you want him to or not. The Holy Spirit, on the other hand, only takes control when you invite Him to and trust Him enough to *allow* Him to be in control.

Having the right perspective on our situations is extremely important to the success and fulfillment of our lives. Without that we can drift from one meaningless endeavor to another, or to one purposeless waste of time and energy after another. Or we can go from one mistake after the other, always coming back to the same problem and same bad habits of thought, feeling, or action. When does it stop? When do we find the breakthrough we need and desire? It's when we begin to see the truth from God's perspective. And that takes God-given discernment.

We need God's perspective on everything, and the only One who can give us that is the Holy Spirit of God whispering to our soul.

Led to Discern God Guiding You

The Holy Spirit is our *guide,* and He wants to guide us in *all* things. He gives us discernment. "The natural man does not receive the things of the Spirit of God, for they are foolishness to him; nor can he know them, because they are spiritually discerned" (1 Corinthians 2:14).

What do you do when you need discernment from God about something specific? First of all, you must be in His Word so much that it is like an intravenous drip constantly sustaining you. Then, of course, praying as much as possible. But for important issues, *fasting and prayer* is a powerful way to seek God's guidance.

It is said of the prophet Ezra that *the hand of God was upon him* (Ezra 7:9). That means he was hearing from God and being led by His Spirit. And God provided what he needed in order to do the work he was called to do — in this case to rebuild the walls around the temple. Ezra *fasted and prayed for guidance,* and he asked the people to also fast and pray for *protection, safety,* and *blessing* on all they were doing (Ezra 8:21–23).

Even the king of Persia recognized that the hand of God was upon Ezra and he was being led by God's Spirit. So he gave Ezra a written decree allowing him to lead the Israelites who were held captive in Persia back to Jerusalem to rebuild the walls of the temple.

When the hand of the Lord is upon you and you are being led by His Spirit, you will find favor from people who recognize something special about you.

Ezra assured the king that because the Lord's hand was upon him he would be protected. But Ezra still *fasted and prayed* for that. When there is a promise from God to you about something specific, and you are being led by His Spirit, you still need to humble yourself in fasting and prayer. You can't presume on God for His protection without any prayer effort. Your part is always to humbly seek God and pray — sometimes with fasting. Even though the Holy Spirit is your guide, you still need to seek guidance.

Fasting and prayer is a sacrifice we make in order to have results we cannot have any other way.

Fast and pray for discernment when the issue is an important one and you cannot afford to make a mistake. How much grief or trouble would we have spared ourselves in the past if we had only done that?

Jephthah was "a mighty man of valor" and the Spirit of the Lord was upon him (Judges

11:1). But as he went to battle against his enemy, he made a hasty and rash vow to the Lord. He said he would sacrifice whatever came out of his house first when he returned home if God would deliver his enemy into his hands (Judges 11:29–31). He did not fast and pray about this extremely important issue.

When Jephthah returned home victorious, his daughter — his only child — came out of his house first. When he saw her, he was distraught because of his vow to the Lord that he could not go back on (Judges 11:34–35). He was not led by the Spirit of God when he made the vow. Now his daughter would never be allowed to marry or bear offspring.

How many times have we made a hasty decision without the leading of the Holy Spirit and something valuable was sacrificed in our lives because of it? Have you ever made a quick choice with your money in order to get something you wanted and then sacrificed financial security as a result? Or ended up with something down the line that was worthless to you? Do you ever look at some of the things you have bought and wish you could have the money back again? We need to pray about everything, and we need to fast when we especially require discernment.

Often prayer and fasting is the only thing that will bring victory. The Israelites wanted to go to war against the wicked tribe of Benjamin, so they asked God for guidance. The Lord told them what to do, but in spite of that they were defeated (Judges 20:21). They prayed again for guidance, weeping before the Lord all day and seeking His counsel, saying, " 'Shall I again draw near for battle against the children of my brother Benjamin?' And the LORD said, 'Go up against him' " (Judges 20:23). Yet again they were defeated. They sought God a third time, *this time with fasting, prayer, weeping,* and *worship* (Judges 20:26). And when they went against Benjamin once more, they were victorious.

This story speaks to us about not giving up. We must not quit seeking God's guidance, even when we experience defeat. We must keep pressing in with *fasting, fervent prayer, humility,* and *worship.*

Why did God tell the Israelites to go ahead to battle the first two times, knowing they would be defeated? He surely had a purpose. Perhaps He was refining them or causing them to be completely dependent on Him. Or perhaps there needed to be a humbling of the people through fasting and prayer. They needed to focus intently on God. There is much we can learn in defeat if we keep our eyes on the Lord and don't give up. When we continue to seek God and become more dependent on Him, we become stronger in faith and He can do great things through us.

To have access to the guidance of the Holy Spirit through God-given discernment and then not follow His leading is a crime against the Spirit. How many times have we gone ahead and done something without seeking the counsel of God because it *seemed* like a good idea at the time? Even when it *appears* right to us, we must still ask God for discernment. Sometimes if we see something we want, we think it must be right. Many of us have done that at one time or another, and too often with dire consequences. Just like children, we each push boundaries as far as we can. How much sugar, chocolate, or french fries would we eat if there were no consequences? How far do we push those boundaries until we learn a hard lesson?

We can also presume that because the Holy Spirit led us to do something one way at one time, He will lead us to do it the same way next time. And we might be wrong. That's why God wants us to stay close to Him, depend on Him, and listen to Him for direction for every step we take.

Young David had great discernment. He knew that Israel's army was the army of God, and he was clear about whose side he was on and who was on his side. David tried to convince the men with King Saul's army that *he* alone should go up against Goliath, the enemy giant. When Saul heard about David's inquiry, he discounted David because of his youth (1 Samuel 17:32–33).

Young people who have received Jesus and have the Holy Spirit in them often have a courageous heart. I think they sometimes hear from God better than an adult who knows too much worldly knowledge and not enough about God's ways. David heard from God, he had the Holy Spirit leading him, and he had the confidence that comes with that. So David convinced Saul that he had what it took to do the job.

Because David knew he had the leading of the Spirit of God, he faced Goliath with only a sling and five smooth stones. He said to Goliath, "You come to me with a sword, with a spear, and with a javelin. But I come to you in the name of the LORD of hosts, the God of the armies of Israel, whom you have defied. This day the LORD will deliver you into my hand, and I will strike you and take your head from you . . . that all the earth may know that there is a God in Israel . . . *for the battle is the LORD's,* and He will give you into our hands" (1 Samuel 17:45–47, emphasis added).

The confrontation happened just as David said it would (1 Samuel 17:50–51). When David killed Goliath, Saul feared David. That's because he recognized God was with David but had left Saul (1 Samuel 18:12).

You know when God is with you. His Spirit gives you confidence and courage — not in yourself, but in the Lord. A person can think their own self-confidence is all they need, but it's not enough. Their confidence must be in God, just as David's was.

Sometimes God will guide you through others, but you need discernment from the Holy Spirit in order to recognize that.

David and his men were staying for a time in Carmel, and they protected some shepherds and their flocks in the area. But when David's men asked the shepherds' wealthy master, Nabal (which means "fool," if that gives you any indication as to his character), to give them food, Nabal not only refused, but he also insulted David. David responded, "Surely in vain I have protected all that this fellow has in the wilderness, so that nothing was missed of all that belongs to him. And he has repaid me evil for good" (1 Samuel 25:21). David planned to take revenge on him, but Nabal's wife, Abigail, upon hearing what David was planning, went to David and pleaded with him not to do what he would regret (1 Samuel 25:22–31).

David discerned that Abigail's advice was *coming from God,* and so he listened, respected what she had to say, and heeded her warning (1 Samuel 25:32–35). When Abigail told her husband what happened, Nabal had a heart attack and died (1 Samuel 25:37–38). When David heard that Nabal was dead, he recognized that God had brought "the wickedness of Nabal on his own head" (1 Samuel 25:39). *He praised God for keeping him from doing the wrong thing in retaliation.*

David heeded the leading of the Lord to his soul through a godly woman, and that spared him from unnecessary bloodshed and a mark against his reputation.

When we fail to hear God guiding us through a godly person He puts into our life, we can lose out on one of our greatest blessings.

When you pray for guidance, be open to the Holy Spirit guiding you through another person He puts in your life. Sometimes you need the information that other person has in order to do the right thing.

Although I mentioned this in chapter 3, it is well worth repeating here, and that is whenever you receive advice from another person that is unsolicited, or you are not sure it is from the Lord, hold it up to the Word of God. Pray about it. See if the Holy Spirit in you bears witness to the rightness of it. Run it by another godly counselor or advisor to see if they believe the advice is from God. Don't move on it without some kind of confirmation to your soul. It should come from a person who serves God and hears from the Holy Spirit in them.

The Holy Spirit will help you discern when God is guiding you through another person.

Invite God to be a part of your life moment by moment. Speak to Him often throughout each day and ask Him to speak to you. Wait for His reply. Arrange to have the time you need to hear from Him. Sometimes He will say, *"Don't go this way, go that way." "Don't leave now, leave later." "Don't buy that, buy this." "Trust this person, not that one."* You may think God doesn't have time for all of these minor details, but He has all the time in the world. If He has time to number the hairs on your head and never leave you or forsake you, then He has time to lead you in all things. God cares about every detail of your life, so don't make decisions without some kind of confirmation to your soul from the Lord about what your decision should be.

The way God may speak to your heart about certain decisions is often by the peace — or lack thereof — you have about it. The best rule to follow is if you don't have total peace about something, don't make a decision until you do, one way or the other. If you need to make a quick decision, however, ask God to show you immediately. He is there instantaneously because His Spirit is in you. And if you have been walking closely with the Lord, communicating with Him daily, asking for discernment and guidance, praying about everything, and staying in His Word, you will hear His voice speak to you even when you don't have time to ask. That's because you have already prayed for wisdom.

PRAYER POWER

Lord, You have said in Your Word that anyone who keeps Your commands will be kept out of harm's way, and in our wisdom from You we can discern much (Ecclesiastes 8:5). I pray You will give me the wisdom to discern the things I need to see. Help me to discern between the righteous and the wicked, and between those people who truly serve You and those who don't, even though they pretend to (Malachi 3:18). Keep me from believing a lie.

Give me discernment to know when the advice I am receiving from someone is actually from You. I don't want to ever miss Your leading because my ears are closed to humbly receiving Your guidance from someone else. Speak to my heart. Lead me in every step I take. I don't want to assume that I always know what's right and miss what You are trying to tell me. Bring into my life godly advisors and people who serve You and who are guided by You. Don't let pride in me cause me to not be humble enough to receive Your guidance in a way I was not expecting. Also, help me to discern when the advice I am getting is *not* from You. Help me to know clearly what You are wanting me to understand. In Jesus' name I pray.

WORD POWER

You shall again discern between the righteous and the wicked, between one who serves God and one who does not serve Him.

MALACHI 3:18

He who keeps his command will experience nothing harmful; and a wise man's heart discerns both time and judgment.

ECCLESIASTES 8:5

Led to Discern God Blessing You

Now, you would think we would recognize when God is blessing us, but this is not always the case. Often we don't even see a blessing when it's right in front of us because it is not the blessing we were expecting. We become focused on our wants and needs and often don't appreciate what God is doing in our lives at that moment. Sometimes we miss it because we think our life is working fine, and we would be surprised to find out that it isn't. God blesses us by saving us from ourselves more often than we know.

There can also be times when we don't think our life is working at all, but it is. We believe things should be a certain way and they are not, so we think God is not blessing us when, in fact, He is. That's why it is absolutely crucial to your success in life that you are able to discern God's blessings on you.

I am talking about godly success here, not worldly success. A truly successful life is one that works the way it is supposed to — where you are becoming all God made you to be without ever violating that, and you are in a close relationship with Him and being led by His Holy Spirit.

The Holy Spirit can help you see your life in the light of eternity and enable you to discern God's blessings now.

Sometimes God will give to you special gifts in your day, and it is good to be able to recognize them. Ask the Holy Spirit to reveal them to you. God will speak to your heart in some way, even if only to say that He loves you. When you can acknowledge a gift from Him in that way, you will receive the affirming, encouraging, and delightful blessing it is meant to be.

When we built our new house, we had to cut down a number of trees. After we moved in, there was a beautiful little redbird that tried every day — many times a day starting early in the morning — to come through the large window in our bathroom. He would sit on the window ledge and peck at the glass, or he would hover next to the glass like a helicopter and fly into it again and again, hitting his beak against it. I was afraid he would knock himself out, but he didn't give up. It was obvious to me that we must have cut down his favorite tree, and he was trying to get through the glass to find his home again.

He was tenacious, to say the least. Early every morning I heard him banging on the window, and that would be my unwelcome daily alarm clock.

It's Red again, I thought. (I cleverly called him "Red.")

It wasn't possible to open the window because the pane of glass was way too large to be anything but stationary, or else I would have opened it and tried to persuade him that there was no tree in our house for him to live in.

Finally, after a couple months of this, my husband put up some birdfeeders in the backyard next to the small waterfall that flowed into the pond at the bottom. We planted three new trees as well — the kind that have beautiful, lacy, pink blossoms in the spring but lose all of their leaves in the winter.

Red finally went to live in one of the trees closest to the biggest birdfeeder. And he ate heartily along with the rest of the little brown, gray, and blue birds that surely had also been misplaced by our rude and sudden cutting down of their homes as well.

For a couple years he was there. Occasionally another redbird would join him on his tree among the birdfeeders, and they would take baths in the little mini pond that formed from the trickling waterfall.

Early one morning in the middle of winter I woke up to a fresh, thick snowfall covering the ground. All of the trees were stark gray limbs with no sign of green anywhere. The sky was also gray and cold, but there was a muted, cloud-covered light from the sun that made the snow white and glistening. I got up to make some hot tea.

In our kitchen, one whole wall facing the backyard is glass. The hillside goes up from the house in the back and provides a great view of the waterfall, trees, birdfeeders, and the pond a few feet from the window. The entire scene, with the sparkling white snow against a backdrop of gray sky and gray leafless trees, was exquisite. I went over to the window to admire it, and there, in Red's favorite tree, must have been 30 to 40 redbirds exactly like him. They were so evenly perched that it was like a Christmas tree decorated with ornaments. It was stunningly beautiful. Breathtaking!

I wanted to call everyone in the house to wake up and look. I wanted to run and get my camera to capture the moment forever. But I couldn't move. I was transfixed. I knew if I left, it would all be gone when I got back.

Where had all these exquisite redbirds come from, converging there in that moment? I knew it was from God. Some things you just know. It was far too astounding to be anything else. Who else could have orchestrated that scene? There was not a bit of color in the entire picture except for the redbirds all in one tree. There weren't any in the other trees. It was beyond imagination. Beyond words. After a minute they all flew away except for Red, and that was the last time I ever saw them. I will never forget it.

Even though it was a profoundly spiritual moment and I knew it was from the Lord, I couldn't figure out what it meant. I thought about the symbolism in the Bible. The Holy Spirit appeared in the form of a white dove.

White represents purity. The color red is symbolic of Christ's blood. And the bare trees were like the starkness of our lives when everything is stripped away. But I still could not grasp the significance of all this. What was God trying to tell me? I asked the Holy Spirit to show me, but I never heard anything about it from Him. I praised God for the spectacular display and kept it in my heart.

A few months later it was spring, and Pastor Jack came to town on a business trip and stayed at our house. He and Anna are always welcome guests. My husband and I were having breakfast with him one morning before his round of early meetings, and we were sitting at the breakfast table looking out over the vivid spring green grass and colorful flowers surrounding the pond and waterfall and the now lavishly blooming pink-blossomed trees. Pastor Jack commented on the beautiful redbird in the tree, and I told him about what happened that one morning in the middle of winter.

"I know that moment was from the Lord," I said. "But I can't figure out the message God was trying to communicate to me. What do you think it is?"

He agreed that it was from God, but he

added, "It was a gift to show His love for you."

I was amazed. That possibility never entered my mind. And I don't believe I would have ever thought of that on my own. *God gave me that wondrous scene as a gift to show His love for me? How can that be?* I wondered.

Looking back on that day now, I remembered I was experiencing an especially hard season of my life just then. I felt sad and discouraged that morning when I got up. And that lovely gift from the Lord was indeed an encouragement to me — reminding me that God had a place of exceptional beauty, rest, and peace in the midst of hard times. Even now, it warms my heart to think about it.

God will bring gifts to you too in the midst of difficult times. But you must be able to identify them as the blessings they are. When we think of blessings, we look for something tangible to hold in our hands, or in our bank account, or something that is specifically identifiable that qualifies as a legitimate blessing. And though the profound sense of His presence is a gift we cannot hold in our hand or deposit in our bank account, we can hold it in our heart forever, and it will be deposited in our mind and soul for a lifetime. It is a priceless jewel, precious beyond all else.

Ask the Holy Spirit to help you discern God's blessings so you can receive them with a grateful heart of worship. Unless you can discern when God is blessing you, you will not be able to show Him the pleasure you have in it.

PRAYER POWER

Lord, I thank You for all of the many blessings You have bestowed upon my life. I know there are those I am not even aware of, and I don't ever want to be ungrateful for them. Give me discernment to see when a situation that I think is inconvenient is actually a blessing from You. Help me to see all the times You have saved me from myself. I thank You that "Your blessing is upon Your people" (Psalm 3:8). Help me to always acknowledge that and give You glory for it. Thank You, Lord, that Your "blessings are on the head of the righteous" (Proverbs 10:6).

Lord, help me to appreciate all that You do for me. I don't want to be so preoccupied that I never take a moment to see and breathe in all You are doing in my life. Give me discernment to see Your hand of blessing to me. I know that when You pour blessings into our lives, they never bring sorrow with them (Proverbs 10:22). Your blessings are pure and beneficial to the heart of those for whom they are intended. I know You bless everyone who fears You and walks in Your way (Psalm 128:1). Help me to show my gratefulness to You for all Your blessings in ways that please You.

In Jesus' name I pray.

WORD POWER

The blessing of the LORD makes one rich, and He adds no sorrow with it.

PROVERBS 10:22

He will bless those who fear the LORD, both small and great.

PSALM 115:13

Led to Discern God Protecting You

How many times has God protected us from evil or danger that we don't even realize, let alone have thanked Him for it? How often has He tried to keep each one of us out of harm's way, but we have not listened to His leading? How many of us are paying a price for not seeking God's will before we made a decision to do something, whether financially, relationally, or in the care of our body? When has He protected us at a time and place where we could have been seriously injured? God protects us far more than we ever realize. We need to be able to discern when God is protecting us so we can cooperate with Him.

Part of God protecting us is *providing* for us as well. We need to discern when God is doing that, because we don't always see it. He provides for us in countless ways, and we don't always give Him the praise He is due.

Apart from the resurrection, the miracle of Jesus feeding the 5000 is the only miracle recorded in all four Gospels. It speaks to us of how the Lord protects us by multiplying what we have in order to meet our needs.

My husband and I were over at a friend's house for dinner one night. She and her husband were always having people to their home for a meal, and this night there were eight of us — the six people who lived in their house and the two of us — actually a small group for them. She had already put the meal on the table buffet-style and we were just getting ready to pray over it when about eight more people came in. She quickly turned to her husband and me and said, "We don't have enough food for this many. Let's pray for God to multiply it." So we quickly prayed together right then and asked God to multiply the food to meet everyone's need. Then we joined hands with everyone else and thanked God for what we were about to receive.

We did not mention this to the new guests, and of course those of us who knew the situation took less food than we would have normally. But that still doesn't account for being able to feed twice as many people and have their hunger fully satisfied. I can still see in my mind what food was there, and it was not nearly enough. Some people might have explained it away, but we did not. We never forgot how God provided by a miracle.

Another example of *God protecting us by providing for us* is the prophet Elisha, who was approached by a God-fearing widow telling him that creditors were coming to take away her two sons to be slaves. Elisha said to her, "Tell me, what do you have in the house?" And she said she had "nothing in the house but a jar of oil" (2 Kings 4:1–2).

Elisha instructed her to borrow empty vessels from her neighbors, but *she was not to gather just a few*. She was to prepare for a larger miracle than she could imagine. When she brought home the vessels, she was told to shut the door (2 Kings 4:3–4). Basically, she was to shut out the doubt of the world.

Elisha told her to pour the oil she had into the vessels, which she did, and it did not stop pouring out until she had run out of containers for it (2 Kings 4:6). The oil stopped pouring out when she filled the last vessel. The widow was then able to sell the oil and pay off her debts. *God used what little she had and multiplied it. He will do the same for you too. God will pour out as much on you as you are able to receive.*

When you are in dire need, seek the leading of the Holy Spirit as to what to do. He may show you what you already have that can be used as a solution to the problem. Or He may do a new thing. In order to prepare for a blessing from God, you must shut the door on doubt. Don't limit what God can do in your situation just because you can't imagine it. His reward may be in proportion to your faith and willingness to receive it. Ask the Holy Spirit to help you discern His provision for you.

God protects us in so many ways and far

more than we know. Ask the Holy Spirit to give you discernment about your life and situations so you can see the ways in which God is protecting you. That will help you to cooperate with Him and not resist Him in any way.

PRAYER POWER

Lord, I thank You for protecting me from the evil plans of the enemy. You are the "the God of my strength, in whom I will trust; my shield and the horn of my salvation, my stronghold and my refuge; my Savior, You save me from violence. I will call upon the LORD, who is worthy to be praised; so shall I be saved from my enemies" (2 Samuel 22:3–4). Thank You for the countless times You have delivered me from trouble I wasn't even aware of. In my distress, I have called on You many times, and You have heard my voice and answered my prayers (2 Samuel 22:7).

I pray You will continue to protect me in everything I do. Thank You that You supply all of my needs, and especially my need for protection. Thank You for all the ways You have protected me in the past, many of which I am not even aware. Thank You in advance for protecting me in the future. I am grateful You have "delivered me from my strong enemy, from those who hated me . . . they confronted me in the day of my calamity," but You, Lord, were "my support." You "brought me out into a broad place;" and delivered me because You "delighted in me" (2 Samuel 22:18–20).

In Jesus' name I pray.

WORD POWER

I will abundantly bless her provision; I will satisfy her poor with bread.

PSALM 132:15

My God shall supply all your need according to His riches in glory by Christ Jesus.

PHILIPPIANS 4:19

10
LED TO PRAY

The Holy Spirit will always lead us to pray. Prayer is foundational in establishing our relationship with God.

God commands us to pray. It is His *will* that we pray. He not only wants us to pray about our own needs, He also wants us to pray about other people and situations. The way God accomplishes His will on the earth is through our prayers. If we are not praying, we are not in His perfect will. Jesus promised that when we pray in His name, power is unleashed to see answers to those prayers. But praying is not telling God what to do. We can tell Him what we *want* Him to do, but we must trust Him to answer our prayers in *His* way and *His* time.

There is more that God wants us to pray about than we can even think of in our minds. That's why He gave us His Spirit to not only lead us to pray, but also *help* us to pray. He will impress upon our heart people and situations we might not think of to pray about on our own.

Paul says that "all things work together for good to those who love God, to those who are the called according to His purpose" (Romans 8:28). But can we just assume that everything is always going to work out for good in every believer's life? Sometimes things don't turn out well. Sometimes terrible things happen to people who love God.

What then?

The verses before verse 28 are talking about prayer. In fact, they are talking about how the Holy Spirit helps us to pray. "*The Spirit also helps in our weaknesses.* For *we do not know what we should pray for* as we ought, but *the Spirit Himself makes intercession for us* with groanings which cannot be uttered" (Romans 8:26, emphasis added). Because we don't always know how to pray as we should, the Holy Spirit will pray through us.

When we are led by the Spirit to pray, He will give the right words to say so our prayers are powerful and effective. Recently I walked through a room where on the television was a live newscast showing a terrible storm about to hit a town in another state. Words of prayer and intercession came out of my mouth, and I knew I was being led by the Holy Spirit to intercede on the town's behalf. As it turned out, that community was spared. I believe God heard the prayers of all who were called as instruments of intercession at that same moment.

Can it be, then, that everything works out for good when we pray? In light of the Scriptures, how can we see it any other way? Working out for good doesn't just automatically happen.

You may wonder why you need to pray when God already knows what you and others need. But He has set it up that way. *We pray,* and *He moves* in response to our prayers. One of the reasons for that is He wants us to depend on Him in every area of our lives so that we will walk closely with Him. He wants us to submit our will to *His.*

The more you pray, the more answers to prayer you will see, and the more your faith will grow. "You, beloved, building yourselves up on your most holy faith, *praying in the Holy Spirit,* keep yourselves in the love of God" (Jude 20–21, emphasis added). "Praying in the Holy Spirit" means you are listening to and guided by the Holy Spirit as you pray. "Building yourself up on your most holy faith" is what happens when you communicate with God in prayer, read His

Word, and then listen for His Spirit to speak to your heart.

Jesus said, "*Ask,* and it will be given to you; *seek,* and you will find; *knock,* and it will be opened to you" (Matthew 7:7, emphasis added). "Ask," "seek," and "knock" are present tense verbs, suggesting that we *keep asking, keep seeking,* and *keep knocking.* These amazing promises of Jesus suggest that all we have to do is ask and it will be given to us. But we all know we don't get everything we ask for when we pray. Why is that? It's because we must ask according to the will of God. If we don't know what the will of God is, we can ask the Holy Spirit to reveal it to us as we pray.

God has promised that we will find what we are seeking, unless what we are seeking goes against His will. He loves us enough to keep us from anything that would not be good for our lives.

We don't just knock once and never again. If the door is not opened, we keep on knocking until God speaks to our heart. What doors are we talking about? It can be a door of opportunity, such as a new job, a new place to live, a new relationship, or a breakthrough in some area of your life. But we can't knock on just any door. Perhaps the door you are knocking on is not God's best for you. Again, you need to be in His Word and asking for the leading of His Spirit. If you are knocking and you still don't have knowledge of the leading of the Lord, say, "Lord, help me to understand how to pray according to Your will."

Led to Pray for the Burdens on Your Heart

Sometimes praying for yourself can be overwhelming. It's often far easier to pray for someone else. We can more clearly see what *their* needs are. Our own needs are often complex, and we can be confused about how to pray. That's why we need the Holy Spirit to help us. There are times when we have such trauma or pain that all we can say is, "God help me," or "God heal me." Sometimes, when the enemy of our soul lies to us, we can be so overwhelmed by the lie that we start to believe him. This depletes us of hope and energy. At those times praying is difficult, and yet it is what we most need to do.

The best news about prayer is that the Holy Spirit not only helps us to pray, but He also strengthens our faith so that we can believe for the answers to our prayers.

When you pray, start with worship and then share the burdens on your heart. They are a heavy weight that needs to be lifted.

Only after you have released those burdens to God can you fully move on to other important things in peace.

The story of Hannah is one of the most beautiful examples of fervent prayer and what God does in response to it. God sometimes allows us to go through difficult times in order to bring us to a point where we are forced to pray fervently in order to see something great happen in our lives.

Hannah, who was barren, made a vow to God and asked Him to give her "a male child," whom she would then give "to the LORD all the days of his life" (1 Samuel 1:11). When Hannah made this vow to God, *she poured out her soul to the Lord* (1 Samuel 1:15). She took her "bitterness of soul" to the Lord in prayer and "wept in anguish" (1 Samuel 1:10). This means her prayers were fervent, exactly the way God wants us to pray. She didn't hang on to bitterness, as she could have, but instead she prayed until she heard from God. This entire story speaks of praying with the leading of the Holy Spirit.

The Lord answered her prayers and gave her a son. She said, "As long as he lives he shall be lent to the LORD" (1 Samuel 1:28). This means she dedicated her child to

God for His services. Her son was Samuel, who became one of the greatest prophets and leaders in all of Israel's history.

Fervent prayer causes great things to happen. Don't be afraid when you are forced to pray fervently because of your circumstances. God is wanting to do something great through you.

PRAYER POWER

Lord, I worship You and thank You that You care about the things that burden my heart. I don't want to carry those things around with me. I want to release them to You in prayer. Specifically, I lift up to You (name your most pressing need). The person I am most concerned about right now is (name the person who you are most concerned about and why). What I want most to see happen right now is (state what you would most like to see happen). Where I most want to see Your power move on my behalf is (name where you would like to see God's power work on your behalf). The most impossible situation I face right now is (name the situation that is impossible for you).

Lord, You have said we don't have what we want because we have not asked

You for it, or have not asked according to Your will (James 4:2–3). Teach me how to pray with the leading of Your Holy Spirit, so that I can pray fervently for what I believe is Your will. Thank You in advance for the answers to these prayers. As I wait on You for the answers, renew my strength and increase my faith (Isaiah 40:31). Only You can lift these burdens from my heart, and I will give You the glory for it.

In Jesus' name I pray.

WORD POWER

You do not have because you do not ask. You ask and do not receive, because you ask amiss, that you may spend it on your pleasures.

JAMES 4:2–3

Those who wait on the LORD shall renew their strength; they shall mount up with wings like eagles, they shall run and not be weary, they shall walk and not faint.

ISAIAH 40:31

Led to Pray for Your Land

Please don't think for a moment that you can skip this section. It is one of the most crucial to your happiness and well-being. A nation from whom God has lifted His hand of protection is horrifying. You don't want to experience it.

Praying for our county is the lowest priority of most people, except for those who have a vision of what will happen if we *don't* pray. I have that vision, and that's why I have put this subject near the top of the list of things to pray for. It must become a *top priority* for us all. This is true for any country, but especially in our country now.

The sin in our land invites God's judgment. Our land was founded on freedom to worship God, and now God has been taken out of everything — schools, public buildings, even malls at Christmas. God is mocked, Jesus is demeaned, and Christians are looked down upon by people who are puffed up with pride against God.

We, God's people, are called to humble ourselves and pray.

God spoke to Solomon saying, "If My people who are called by My name will *humble themselves, and pray* and *seek My face,* and *turn from their wicked ways,* then *I will hear* from heaven, and *will forgive their sin* and *heal their land*" (2 Chronicles 7:14, emphasis added). We must memorize these powerful instructions from God until they are etched in our hearts. We are in the situation we are in now because people did not pray. Yes, many people *have* prayed, and thank God they did or we would not have the blessings we do today. But things will get much worse if the church does not wake up to the call of God to intercede for our nation.

If you are praying for your country, you are being led by the Holy Spirit.

God always allows us to get to the point where we know with certainty that we cannot accomplish what needs to happen on our own. God wants the glory for what He accomplishes. For us to take any credit in any way only contributes to our own pride, which will be our downfall. We set ourselves up for calamity in our land when there is rampant sin and idol worship. When people worship idols, God says, "Let your idols protect you then" and He lifts His hand of protection (Judges 10:14). The only reason He has not done that is because people are praying now.

If we don't pray, we will be guilty of the consequences. When we live our lives dependent upon the Holy Spirit as He leads us to pray, God is glorified and we are saved from ourselves.

PRAYER POWER

Lord, I pray that we, Your people, will hear Your call to humble ourselves and pray for our nation. Give us hearts that are repentant for the sins of our nation and help us to turn from our wicked ways. On behalf of the people in America, I repent before You for the sins of slavery, pornography, child sexual abuse, murder, thievery, greed, selfishness, immorality, rejection of God, sexual sins, murder, the killing of our children, and the rejection of God from our schools, public buildings, and arenas. The stench of our wickedness and perversion must be abhorrent to You. Help us to seek Your face and turn from our evil and wicked ways, so You will hear from heaven and heal our land (2 Chronicles 7:14).

I confess on behalf of all believers our faithlessness, prayerlessness, and refusal to be repentant. Forgive us, Lord, for battling one another over minor disagreements instead of being united in our prayers and quest to see Your will done on earth. Help us to be indignant over what the enemy is doing. Help us to be repentant over our laziness in prayer and for our preoccupations that have allowed him to gain so much ground. Help us to have a passion to see Your will done. Enable us to be led by Your Holy Spirit to rise up in prayer and take our country back so it can once again be a nation whose God is the Lord. In Jesus' name I pray.

WORD POWER

I set watchmen over you, saying, "Listen to the sound of the trumpet!" But they said, "We will not listen."

JEREMIAH 6:17

Open the gates, that the righteous nation which keeps the truth may enter in. You will keep him in perfect peace, whose mind is stayed on You, because he trusts in You.

ISAIAH 26:2–3

Led to Pray for Others

The Holy Spirit will always lead you to pray for other people. When you are praying for the known needs of others, God's Spirit will speak to you specifically about those people and situations. He may bring to your mind something you would have never thought to pray about on your own. Or you may find yourself interceding for people you don't even know, because the Holy Spirit has put them on your heart. When He does that, be continually available for Him to show you how He wants you to pray. Say, "Holy Spirit, reveal to me how You want me to pray for this person right now." Then pray for whatever He brings to your mind, "praying always with all prayer and supplication in the Spirit, being watchful to this end with all perseverance and supplication for all the saints" (Ephesians 6:18).

Have you ever been led to pray for someone — even someone you didn't know personally — and you are surprised by your own fervency, tears, or travail as you pray? I have had that happen many times, and if you have become serious about interceding for others, I'm sure you have as well. That means you are being led by the Holy Spirit to pray for them. The tears are part of the travail, part of the fervency. They are not conjured up. They surface from deep within, initiated by the Holy Spirit in you who sees your heart open to His leading. Actually, you cannot stop them.

There will be many times in your life when someone will come to your mind whom you may not know well or know at all, but because you are a believer and you have the Holy Spirit in you, you cannot ignore that. The reason they have come to your mind is so you can pray for them.

You don't have to devote a long time to praying for someone who comes to mind. It could be just a few sentences as the Lord leads. However, you may find the Holy Spirit leading you to pray longer and more fervently than you thought you would. I have had that happen many times. Sometimes I didn't know why, but other times I'd find out later there was good reason for it. All I am saying is don't ignore this. To not pray when the Holy Spirit is calling you to would be a sin against God. You don't know how many lives you may save by praying for someone God puts on your heart.

Don't forget to pray for strangers. God said we are to love strangers (Deuteronomy 10:19). And I have often been led to pray for strangers. No matter where I am, God will quicken my heart about someone I see for whom He wants me to pray.

Have you ever been in a room of people you don't know and one person will stand out to you for some reason? You might have some kind of concern for them. I don't mean the eyes of strangers meeting across a crowded room, but rather experiencing a certain caring about that person. If that ever happens to you, ask the Holy Spirit how to pray for that man or woman. Or whenever you are around people, ask the Lord to show you if there is someone there for whom He wants you to pray. I doubt He will ever say, "No, definitely not!"

People everywhere you go need prayer, but don't feel you have to pray for every stranger you see. I've been there and tried to do that. Believe me, it's exhausting. But God may quicken your heart to pray for a certain stranger, and when He does you need to heed His prompting.

I know an author named River Jordan. Don't you love that name? She has taken the concept of praying for strangers to a new level that only someone who is called and directed by the Holy Spirit could do. She felt led to pray for one stranger a day for a year. She skillfully relates her experiences in a book called *Praying for Strangers*. Most of us cannot find 365 strangers in a year unless we go out and search for them. But River did that. You don't have to go that far, so don't be intimidated by what she did.

Be *inspired* by it. The Bible says that whatever we do for our brothers and sisters in Christ we are to do for strangers as well (3 John 5). And haven't we all been a stranger in need of prayer at one time or another? Can you envision the ripple effect of good if we were all to pray this way? We may have to get to heaven before we find out the ramifications of those prayers, but we can feel good that we obeyed God and loved the stranger among us.

Pray for anyone who affects your life. There are countless people who affect your life every day, and for the most part, you don't know them personally and will likely never meet them. God tells us in His Word to pray for all those in authority. That means praying for the leaders in our country — from the president to senators, congressmen, governor, mayor, and state representatives. Pray also for protection of the military, police, and firefighters who protect you. Pray for your boss or whoever is over you. Pray for your pastor, other pastors, and their families.

The list of people who affect your life is long, but don't let that overwhelm you. Ask the Holy Spirit to show you who affects your life right now — or will in the future — and needs your prayers. You may not even realize who that might be until the Holy Spirit reveals it to you. And you may never know what is at stake if you don't pray.

Do you understand that whatever peace, safety, or prosperity you are experiencing now is because people are praying?

Manasseh, Hezekiah's son, was an evil king who reigned after Hezekiah. He was Judah's longest-reigning ruler and the most wicked of all of them. Why should the worst ruler reign the longest, except that there were so many people around him who were just as wicked as he was and they obviously did not try to stop him? His evilness had perhaps spread to the people, and they did not pray fervently for his removal.

We, the people, end up paying a price for corrupt and evil leaders. We must pray they will be removed so that good and godly people can take their place. And we must continue to pray for godly people to be raised up and prepared to lead. I believe our prayers for our leaders to serve God have never been more needed than they are today. Pray for your city or community. You don't know what possible disaster is looming around the corner if you don't.

PRAYER POWER

Lord, help me to pray powerfully for the people in my life whom I deeply care about. Bring to mind my family members, friends, coworkers, people at church, and those whom I see as acquaintances whenever they need special prayer. Lead me, Holy Spirit, as I pray for each one according to Your will. Help me to recognize when You have put someone on my heart for whom I should pray. I pray for all those who affect my life, either financially, in my work, in my neighborhood, or in our government. Show me anyone I need to pray for who affects my life in more ways than I can think of now. Jesus, You have said that whatever we ask in Your name, our Father God will do (John 16:23–24). Help me to pray according to Your will.

Lord, I pray that no matter where I am, You would make me aware of someone around me who needs my prayers. I know that we are all "strangers and pilgrims on the earth" (Hebrews 11:13). But as believers we are "no longer strangers and foreigners, but fellow citizens with the saints and members of the household of God" (Ephesians 2:19). I am glad I belong to Your family,

317

Lord, and I have a heart especially for those who don't have that. Help me to know who those people are and how to pray for them.

In Jesus' name I pray.

WORD POWER

I exhort first of all that supplications, prayers, intercessions, and giving of thanks be made for all men, for kings and all who are in authority, that we may lead a quiet and peaceable life in all godliness and reverence. For this is good and acceptable in the sight of God our Savior.

1 TIMOTHY 2:1–3

Bear one another's burdens, and so fulfill the law of Christ.

GALATIANS 6:2

Led to Pray for Miracles

Jesus prayed for miracles, and He told us *we* could do that too. How many times does God want us to pray for a miracle and we don't do it because either we can't find faith to believe for one or we are not sensitive to the leading of the Spirit? Some people insist that miracles don't happen today, and for them I'm sure they don't. Some people don't recognize a miracle even when they see one.

Just because God doesn't work a miracle immediately when they pray, some people think He never will. We don't tell God what to do, but we can limit what God *wants* to do. Just because He doesn't jump to our commands and do a miracle immediately doesn't mean He won't work a miracle in the situation.

Miracles are not on *our* terms; they are on *His*. We must open our eyes to see the real miracles in our lives and give God praise and thanks for them. The more we recognize daily miracles, the greater the miracles we will see.

The prophet Elijah was led to go to a certain city where God had commanded someone to provide for him there. She was a poor widow who had nothing. Now, God could have given Elijah a wealthy person to provide for him, someone who had a lavish guesthouse and room service, but that's not the way God does things. He will put you in situations where you absolutely must have a miracle. The reason He does that is because He wants you to know with all certainty that it is *Him* working in your life.

So don't be alarmed if the Spirit leads you into situations that are impossible without a miracle from God.

The widow told him, "I do not have bread, only a handful of flour in a bin, and a little oil in a jar; and see, I am gathering a couple of sticks that I may go in and prepare it for myself and my son, that we may eat it, and die" (1 Kings 17:12). She was down to the end of her supply. But Elijah said to her, "Do not fear; go and do as you have said, but make me a small cake from it first, and bring it to me; and afterward make some for yourself and your son" (1 Kings 17:13).

The widow followed the leading of the Lord and gave to Elijah, even though she and her son did not have enough for themselves. And just as God said, they did not run out of food (1 Kings 17:16). It was a miracle.

Later, the widow's son became ill and died. Elijah prayed fervently for a miracle because he *believed that God was able to resurrect the child. He could have just helped the widow bury the child, but he was led to pray for the impossible instead.* Only someone who was led by the Spirit of God would know to do that. "The LORD heard the voice of Elijah; and the soul of the child came back to him, and he revived" (1 Kings 17:22).

When you pray for a miracle, the Holy Spirit can give you a surge of faith to believe that a miracle can happen. But you must reject everyone else's unbelief and remain sensitive to His leading in every situation. It could be that the miracle you are requesting is not God's will in this situation.

Don't be afraid when a difficult situation happens. Instead, ask God if there is a miracle He wants to work in it, and ask the Holy Spirit to show you how to pray.

If Jesus did not do miracles when there was doubt and unbelief in the people around Him, how can we expect to see answers to our prayers if we pray around those who have no faith? (Matthew 13:58). We must be around people of faith if we want to see miracles happen in response to our prayers. Miracles have everything to do with faith in God's ability to do one. It has nothing to do with our demanding a miracle and everything to do with following the leading of the Holy Spirit as you pray. Miracles do not occur on demand. They are revealed by God as something He wants, and He looks for someone with faith enough to pray as He instructs.

PRAYER POWER

Lord, help me to learn to pray with the leading of Your Spirit so that I can pray in power to see miracles happen. May the fullness of Your Spirit in me enable me to ask for great things from You as You reveal them to me. Give me strong faith to pray and wait expectantly for a miracle. I don't ever want to be the one who blocks the way for a miracle by my unbelief and prayerlessness. Help me to hear Your voice leading me so that I never ask for something too small in comparison to what You want to see accomplished. Keep my faith strong and free from doubt.

Increase my faith to believe for what seems impossible. You have said in Your Word that all things are possible to him who believes (Mark 9:23). Help me to have faith enough to believe for many miracles. Help me to recognize the miracles You work in my life every day — how You have protected me, led me away from danger, provided for me, and saved me from so much more than I even realize. Teach me how to move in strong faith to see answers to my prayers for miracles. You have said that fervent prayers accomplish a great deal. Help me to pray with conviction and power.

WORD POWER

Most assuredly, I say to you, he who believes in Me, the works that I do he will do also; and greater works than these he will do, because I go to My Father.

JOHN 14:12

Jesus said to him, "If you can believe, all things are possible to him who believes."

MARK 9:23

Led to Pray for Healing

Jesus has power over all disease. "Jesus went about . . . healing all kinds of sickness and all kinds of disease among the people" (Matthew 4:23).

When God told King Hezekiah it was time for him to die, he immediately humbled himself and prayed to God to let him live. He said, "Remember now, O LORD, I pray, how I have walked before You in truth and with a loyal heart, and have done what was good in Your sight" (2 Kings 20:3). And Hezekiah wept. Having previously obeyed God and persisted in prayer, he was miraculously healed by the Lord. God even gave him a sign that He would heal him by making a sundial go back by ten degrees — an impossible miracle. As a result of Hezekiah's prayers, God gave him fifteen more years to live.

This story shows that it is never wrong to pray for a miracle of healing, even in the face of death. God instructed that a poultice of figs be put on Hezekiah — a medical approach at that time — but it is still clear that God was the healer. God asks us to do certain things so that we will show our submission to Him by responding as He has asked us to.

It is clear from Scripture that Jesus healed. But was it capricious on His part? Did He only heal when He felt like it? Or was it more? Scripture makes clear that healing is provided for us because of Jesus' suffering, death, and resurrection on the cross. The Bible says Jesus "took our infirmities and bore our sicknesses" (Matthew 8:17). Divine healing is part of Jesus' redemptive work accomplished by His death and resurrection on the cross and "by whose stripes you were healed" (1 Peter 2:24). Jesus suffered for our sins — yours and mine — and He suffered for our sicknesses.

Having faith in God and His ability to heal will

bring healing to us. A woman who had a flow of blood for 12 years touched the hem of Jesus' garment, believing that if she touched Him she would be healed. When He saw that she was the one who had touched Him, He said, " 'Be of good cheer, daughter; *your faith has made you well.*' And the woman was made well from that hour" (Matthew 9:22, emphasis added). Jesus rewards our faith with healing.

Faith is a gift from God, and we must thank Him for the faith we have and pray that He will increase it.

We must ask God for healing and have faith in His ability to do it. A blind man named Bartimaeus let nothing stop him from getting to Jesus because he believed Jesus could give him sight. Jesus knew what he needed, but He wanted to hear it from Bartimaeus. After he told Jesus what he wanted, Jesus said, " 'Go your way; *your faith has made you well.*' And immediately he received his sight" (Mark 10:51–52, emphasis added).

Some things will not happen in our lives unless we fast and pray about them. Jesus' disciples asked Him why they could not do some of the things *He* did — in this particular case to cure someone who needed to be set free. Jesus explained, "Because of your unbelief; for assuredly, I say to you, if you have faith as a mustard seed, you will say to this mountain, 'Move from here to there,' and it will move; and nothing will be impossible for you. However, this kind does not go out except by prayer and fasting" (Matthew 17:20–21).

There is no substitute for faith, but if we *fast and pray* there is greater power. We must fast and pray in order to break through certain realms of darkness. Jesus said, "I will give you the keys of the kingdom of heaven, and whatever you *bind* on earth will be bound in heaven, and whatever you *loose* on earth will be loosed in heaven" (Matthew 16:19, emphasis added). This has to do with forbidding and permitting. *"Binding"* is *forbidding or stopping. "Loosing"* is *permitting or releasing.*

"Keys" means *"authority."* Jesus gave authority to believers to *stop* things and *release* things. In prayer we can stop something that is happening or keep a bad thing *from* happening.

All that being said, what about the people who are *not* healed? Does God randomly heal some and not others? What about two of the most famous Christian women who have not been healed of their specific conditions?

I am talking about Joni Erickson Tada,

who has been a quadriplegic since she was 17. And Jennifer Rothschild, who was diagnosed with a degenerative eye disease when she was 15 that caused her to become blind not long after that. Immeasurable intercession has gone on for their healing since the day they first needed it. Why did God not answer those prayers?

I have the privilege of knowing both of these women of God, and I can tell you that it is not for lack of faith that they haven't been healed. There is exceptionally strong faith in both of them and in the people all over the world who have prayed for them. It is not for lack of prayer, for prayers have gone up on their behalf all over the planet. It is not because they don't deserve healing, for I have not known any more deserving than they are. Besides, Jesus doesn't heal because people deserve it. He heals because He loves them. Does that mean Jesus doesn't love Joni and Jennifer? Far from it. He loves them completely and unconditionally.

I don't know why He has not healed them — and I am not saying He won't — but He has chosen not to for His purposes. He has used them powerfully in this world and will continue to do so in the future. The two of them are responsible for many changes which have allowed people in similar situations to have a better life. There is also a quality about both of them that is beyond what is common. It is a supernatural glow from the Lord, and it is stunning. While they are both naturally beautiful, they each have a beauty that is more than earthly beauty. God has given them a portion of *His beauty* to reside in them. It is undeniable. And they are both humble enough not to recognize it in themselves. But when I am in their presence, I sense the presence of God. They are an inspiration to all who know them or know about them. No one represents Him better.

I don't like that they are not healed, and I will continue to pray for that. But God has and is using them powerfully to bring hope to others. I can't count the times they have been an inspiration to me, and there are countless others who have read their books and heard them speak who feel the same way. They help us to keep going and not lose heart when times get tough and God has not answered our prayers. It may be that their ultimate healing will be in heaven when they see Jesus. But I know their reward for fruitful service will be great and they will rejoice for eternity, for they touched the world powerfully and made a profound difference in the lives of all who knew them.

If you have prayed and prayed and have not been healed, it could be that God is using you, too, to be an encouragement to others to not give up. The Holy Spirit in you can make a difference in all who are around you, no matter what condition you are in. Always pray for healing, but know that God has the final say on whom He heals.

PRAYER POWER

Lord, I pray that Your Holy Spirit will manifest Himself in power in my life so that I can pray for people to be healed and they will be. Help me to intercede when people are bound by the enemy of their soul and they need to be set free. Move through me when I pray for others as Your Spirit leads me. Hear my prayers when I pray for myself, my family, and people I know who need Your healing touch. I never want to glorify myself in the process, but I do want so much to glorify You.

Lord, I don't understand why some people are healed and others are not, but I trust You. Even though I want everyone who is prayed for and who has faith in You to be healed, I know You use people who are not healed in miraculous ways. Help me to trust You on that. Help *them* to trust You too. Lead me to pray for healing no matter what happens. Show me whom to pray for and how to pray for them. Teach me to pray the way You want me to and how Your Holy Spirit leads me. Use me as an instrument for Your healing power. Thank You, Jesus, that on the cross You "took our infirmities" and "bore our sicknesses" (Matthew 8:17). I thank You always and forever for what You have done for me.

In Jesus' name I pray.

WORD POWER

Is anyone among you suffering? Let him pray. Is anyone cheerful? Let him sing psalms. Is anyone among you sick? Let him call for the elders of the church, and let them pray over him, anointing him with oil in the name of the Lord. And the prayer of faith will save the sick, and the Lord will raise him up.

JAMES 5:13–15

Confess your trespasses to one another, and pray for one another, that you may be healed. The effective, fervent prayer of a righteous man avails much.

JAMES 5:16

Led to Pray for as Long as It Takes

When you are praying for something important, don't give up and stop praying before the Holy Spirit leads you to.

The Angel of the Lord appeared to the barren wife of Manoah and told her she would conceive and bear a son. She was not to drink wine or eat anything unclean, and she was never to allow her son's hair to be cut. That's because he would be a Nazirite — someone who takes a vow of consecration to the Lord — and he would deliver Israel from the hands of the Philistines (Judges 13:2–7).

When the child was born, they named him Samson. As he grew, *"the Spirit of the LORD began to move upon him"* (Judges 13:25, emphasis added). The Lord empowered him by His Holy Spirit and prepared him to deliver Israel.

Often in the seemingly barren times in our lives — when there has been unanswered prayer for a long time — if we will keep praying and not give up, our prayers will eventually be answered with something great. They may not be answered the way

331

we thought, but God *will* answer. The Bible contains many instances of women who agonized over their inability to conceive. Their prayers for a child go unanswered for an *unbearably* long time, until one day the Holy Spirit reveals that they will not only conceive, but they will bear a child who will be used mightily of God. Besides Samson, other examples in the Bible of children for whom their mothers prayed fervently are Joseph, Samuel, and John the Baptist — each one a child of promise.

If you have been seeking God for the realization of a particular dream you've had for a long time, God will put a word in your heart about it. If the dream is from Him, you will feel deeply that it is God's will and you will have peace. Keep on praying and don't give in to discouragement, and you will eventually give birth to that promise.

If the dream in your heart is *not* God's will for your life, He will reveal that to you when you ask Him to. Be willing to lay the dream at the feet of God and surrender it to Him. He will take away your desire for it and give you a dream that is far greater. Listen to the Holy Spirit speaking to your heart about that. You don't want to go around with a dream in your heart that God won't bless.

When you believe what you are praying for is from God, hold fast to that. Even when things happen to discourage you from believing that it will ever happen, continue to hold tight to the promise God has put in you. The fact that you must pray and wait for so long only means God wants to do something great. And that takes much fervent intercession to accomplish. Also, God will wait until you have absolutely no doubt that it is He who will accomplish it. You will be convinced it could not happen any other way. God promises you a good future and a reason to hope. Don't give up on that.

When you become discouraged, pray more. When it seems as though God will never bring forth what you are seeking, refuse to give up. When it appears as if nothing will ever happen, fast and pray again.

God doesn't always answer our prayers the way we pray them. That's where faith comes in. Often people give up and stop praying too quickly. If their prayers aren't answered right away, they think God doesn't hear or care. I know people who turned away from God because their prayers weren't answered, as if He was the great sugar daddy in the sky who existed only to give them what they wanted. So they were willing to sacrifice all that God had for them, which would have been far greater than what they dreamed for themselves, because God didn't give them what they wanted at that time.

Be sensitive to the Spirit when it comes to prayer. Keep praying for as long as it takes in order to get an answer one way or another.

PRAYER POWER

Lord, I pray You will help me to not give up praying when I don't see answers to my prayers right away, or because my prayers are not answered exactly the way I prayed them. Regarding the things that are most pressing on my heart, enable me to pray for as long as it takes. For other things that are not as pressing, each time after I pray, help me to release the matter into Your hands. Give me the wisdom to know how to pray. Help me to understand whether You have not answered those prayers *yet,* or You are not going to answer them the way I prayed them. Lead me, Holy Spirit, as I pray so that I can understand *how* to pray.

Help me to not grow weary in doing good, for I know that "in due season we shall reap if we do not lose heart" (Galatians 6:9). I know that I want to see answers to my prayers now, and it is hard to wait, but I put my trust in You and Your perfect timing. Thank You that You always hear and always answer — in Your way and Your time. I have set You always before me, Lord, and because You are with me, I shall not give up (Psalm 16:8).

In Jesus' name I pray.

WORD POWER

He spoke a parable to them, that men always ought to pray and not lose heart.

LUKE 18:1

Take up the whole armor of God, that you may be able to withstand in the evil day, and having done all, to stand. Stand therefore, having girded your waist with truth, having put on the breastplate of righteousness.

EPHESIANS 6:13–14

11
LED TO FOLLOW GOD

The Holy Spirit will always lead you to follow hard after God. You will find your soul yearning for more of Him. You will want His Word engraved in your heart. You will have a longing to be closer to Him that will give you a never-ceasing passion for His presence.

It is amazing that after all God had done for the Israelites with many signs in Egypt — turning water into blood; the onslaught of frogs, lice, flies, disease, boils, hail, locusts, and darkness; the death of the firstborn Egyptians; and the Israelites being set free from slavery while carrying with them the silver and gold of the Egyptians — they *still doubted God* and rebelled against Him.

How could the children of Israel forget when they walked across the Red Sea on dry land while the Egyptian army chased after them into the sea and drowned? How could they doubt God after He provided for them every day in the wilderness? Their clothes didn't wear out for 40 years (Deuteronomy 8:4). How could they not remember His works?

It's not that they *couldn't* remember; they chose *not* to. They wanted what they wanted. "They soon *forgot His works;* they *did not wait for His counsel.* But *lusted exceedingly* in the wilderness, and *tested God* in the desert" (Psalm 106:13–14, emphasis added). "They *forgot God their Savior,* who had done great things in Egypt" (Psalm 106:21, emphasis added). As a result of not wanting to follow God's leading, they had to stay in the wilderness for years.

When God brought the Israelites into a good land, rich with all they could possibly want, He warned them that if they forgot Him and His ways, and stopped living by His commandments, they would be destroyed (Deuteronomy 8:11–20). Yet they still persisted in wanting to do things *their way* and not follow *God.* So He gave them what they wanted "but sent leanness into their soul" (Psalm 106:15).

We are a lot like the Israelites. We often want things that are not God's will for us, and we become empty when we have too much and don't follow Him.

Why is it that when we as a people have plenty of food, a place to live, and our needs are met, we tend to forget God? We don't pray as much because we don't need as much. We don't read the Word as much because we are too busy and we think we can rely on our memory. We say, as they did, that the power and might of our hands have gained us what we have, instead of remembering that it is *God* who gives us the power to prosper (Deuteronomy 8:18).

King Asa, early in his reign, took down the high places and the altars of worship to false gods. He commanded the people to seek the Lord and live according to His ways. When things were good and they were no longer at war, he said, " 'Let us build these cities and make walls around them, and towers, gates, and bars, while the land is yet before us, because *we have sought the LORD our God; we have sought Him, and He has given us rest on every side.*' So they built and prospered" (2 Chronicles 14:7, emphasis added).

When there was peace and prosperity in the land, the people didn't become fat and lazy. Instead, they *sought the Lord* and *used the time to rebuild and strengthen.* We must remember to do that too. When things are good in your life, take the time to build and fortify your relationship with God. Whether you are in good times or bad, follow Him to an even deeper place.

Led to Follow God to an Intimate Day-by-Day Walk with Him

Every day the Holy Spirit will lead you to an intimate walk with Him. And He will work on you so that your heart is clean before Him. You don't have to be perfect, but your heart must be right. You can't live your life doing *what* you want, *when* you want; you must be submitted to the leading of the Holy Spirit. That doesn't mean *any* spirit, because there are others and you definitely don't want to be led by them. They are not holy. They are not God. They don't have your best interests at heart. And they will lead you in the opposite direction of where you want to be going in your life.

When you live by God's laws and walk day by day, moment by moment with the Holy Spirit, you will always be headed in the right direction. And it is not difficult, because He does all the heavy lifting. When you lift Him up in praise, He lifts you up in every other way. He becomes your *strength* when you have none. He is your *guide* when you don't know what to do. He is your *comforter* when you are hurting and distressed. I am not saying you will never have another problem when you are led by the Spirit, because we don't always follow Him perfectly. And Jesus said there will be times of suffering, but He will be with you in them.

We all have a tendency to bring suffering upon ourselves needlessly because we want to take complete control of our lives and not allow the Holy Spirit to perfect us. Paul said, "Are you so foolish? *Having begun in the Spirit, are you now being made perfect by the flesh?*" (Galatians 3:3, emphasis added).

He wants you to live a life where you can accomplish things that could not happen if He were not enabling you to do it — a life where you know that if He doesn't come through for you, you are ruined. And it seems scary to live that way. But, actually, it is scarier to *not* live that way. To live apart from His power, wisdom, and guidance is frightening.

God wants us to live a life we cannot possibly live without Him.

When King Saul stopped following God and became obsessed with trying to kill David, the Holy Spirit left him. When he inquired of the Lord, and God did not answer him, Saul sought a medium to bring up the spirit of the prophet Samuel from the dead. Samuel told Saul it was because of his disobedience to God that the Holy Spirit had left him (1 Samuel 38:3–20). We can fall off the path God has for us too if we don't make a deliberate effort to walk closely with Him every day.

Be careful how you walk. Make the most of your time and use it wisely. Don't waste it. Be productive. Don't let God just be there; interact with Him. Walk so closely with Him that you hear His heartbeat. Pray. Listen. Seek the leading of His Holy Spirit. Begin every day with God — in prayer, in His Word, and in worship — so that no matter what arises, you are more than ready.

PRAYER POWER

Lord, I pray You would draw me closer and help me to establish a solid day-by-day walk with You. Purify my soul and help me to obey You in every way, beginning with my thoughts and attitudes. I don't want anything in my life that separates me from You. Keep me from trying to live my life doing only what *I* want instead of what *You* want. I don't ever want to pay the price for being apathetic about following Your leading. I know the only way to find true peace is to live in obedience to You.

Help me to "walk worthy" of You, pleasing You, being fruitful in every good work, and "increasing in the knowledge" of You (Colossians 1:10). Help me to "walk in the newness of life" that You, Jesus, died for me to have (Romans 6:4). Enable me to "walk within my house with a perfect heart" (Psalm 101:2). Help me to set aside time each day to spend with You alone, as a priority I never neglect. I want to meet You in Your Word daily and see greater manifestations of Your presence. Help me to know You better every day. Enable me to live a life that is not possible without You.

In Jesus' name I pray.

WORD POWER

If anyone serves Me, let him follow Me; and where I am, there My servant will be also. If anyone serves Me, him My Father will honor.

JOHN 12:26

As you therefore received Christ Jesus the Lord, so walk in Him, rooted and built up in Him and established in the faith, as you have been taught, abounding in it with thanksgiving.

COLOSSIANS 2:6–7

Led to Follow God to Purify the Words You Speak

When you give the Holy Spirit free rein in your life, He will clean house on your soul. He's not going to move into an unpleasant home of chaos and sin without doing something about it. The only reason He can dwell there at all is because God sees the righteousness of Jesus in you. He knows when your thoughts and actions are not consistent with who God made you to be.

God not only demands purity of heart but also the most obvious manifestation of a pure heart, which is purity of speech. In fact, He won't tolerate anything less. The Holy Spirit will cause the words of your mouth to torment you if you violate God's clear directives about them in His Word.

Our hearts and words must be aligned with God so that we speak with our mouths what God has put in our hearts by the power of His Holy Spirit.

The Bible says, "Let each one of you *speak truth* with his neighbor" because we are joined with each other (Ephesians 4:25, emphasis added). "Let *no corrupt word* proceed out of your mouth, but what is *good for necessary edification,* that it may *impart grace* to the hearers . . . Let all . . . *evil speaking* be put away from you" (Ephesians 4:29,31, emphasis added).

Jesus said that it is "not what goes into the mouth defiles a man; but what comes out of the mouth, this defiles a man" (Matthew 15:11). *"For out of the heart proceed evil thoughts"* (Matthew 15:19, emphasis added). We are defiled by what we speak. And what happens in our mind and heart determines whether good or evil comes out of our mouth.

Our words will always reveal the condition of our heart. When we speak words that are unkind, deceptive, or faithless, it indicates we have heart problems.

TEN THINGS THE BIBLE SAYS ABOUT THE WORDS WE SPEAK

1. **Words of gossip destroy.** "A perverse man sows strife, and a whisperer separates the best of friends" (Proverbs 16:28).
2. **Words that are careless bring destruction.** "He who guards his mouth preserves his life, but he who

opens wide his lips shall have destruction" (Proverbs 13:3).

3. **Words must be kind and forgiving.** "Be kind to one another, tenderhearted, forgiving one another, even as God in Christ forgave you" (Ephesians 4:32).

4. **Words must edify.** "Let no corrupt word proceed out of your mouth, but what is good for necessary edification, that it may impart grace to the hearers" (Ephesians 4:29).

5. **Words bring health.** "There is one who speaks like the piercings of a sword, but the tongue of the wise promotes health" (Proverbs 12:18).

6. **Words must be true.** "A false witness will not go unpunished, and he who speaks lies will not escape" (Proverbs 19:5).

7. **Words bring strength.** "The Lord God has given Me the tongue of the learned, that I should know how to speak a word in season to him who is weary. He awakens Me morning by morning, He awakens My ear to hear as the learned" (Isaiah 50:4).

8. **Words of complaint are against God's ways.** "Do all things without

complaining and disputing" (Philippians 2:14).

9. **Words can set a trap for us.** "You are snared by the words of your mouth; you are taken by the words of your mouth" (Proverbs 6:2).

10. **Words can bring death into a situation.** "Death and life are in the power of the tongue, and those who love it will eat its fruit" (Proverbs 18:21).

Our words matter more than we think. We create our own world with the words we say. The Holy Spirit will never lead you to speak badly of God, yourself, or anyone else. And every careless word we say will have to be accounted for one day before God (Matthew 12:36). What a frightening thought! If you want to stop any negative speech, deliberately speak the Word of God. There is a correlation between being filled with the Holy Spirit and speaking God's Word with boldness (Acts 4:31). When the Holy Spirit leads you to speak God's Word with boldness, you won't want to go back to any negative speech habits.

Lord, fill my heart with Your love, peace, and joy so that what comes out of my mouth represents Your will. I pray the overflow of my heart will cause me to always speak words that bring life and not destruction. Help me to do all things without complaining. I have decided that my mouth will not sin (Psalm 17:3). "Let the words of my mouth and the meditation of my heart be acceptable in Your sight, O LORD, my strength and my Redeemer" (Psalm 19:14).

Lord, show me when I say negative things about myself or others. Help me to not speak words that grieve You. Keep me from faithless words. Help me to follow Your leading so that I never say things that hurt others. Pour Your Spirit afresh into my heart each day so that what I say reflects *Your* nature. I know that "the lips of the righteous know what is acceptable, but the mouth of the wicked what is perverse" (Proverbs 10:32). Give me the right words at all times. Keep my mouth from ever saying anything that is not gracious or kind. Give me "the tongue of the learned, that I should know how to speak a word in season to him who is weary" (Isaiah

50:4). Help me to edify and bless others with the words I speak.

In Jesus' name I pray.

WORD POWER

Out of the abundance of the heart the mouth speaks.

MATTHEW 12:34

He who would love life and see good days, let him refrain his tongue from evil, and his lips from speaking deceit.

1 PETER 3:10

Led to Follow God to Mountain-Moving Steps of Faith

The Holy Spirit in you will always lead you toward ever-increasing steps of faith. Jesus said that with strong faith in Him, it is possible to move mountains. That may not mean you will move the mountain in your backyard to some other place, but you can move other mountain-size obstacles in your life. Obstacles in your relationships, marriage, finances, health, mind, or emotions, or whatever presents itself, can be moved.

Faith speaks to something you don't yet see as if it has already happened. What looks like defeat will become a major victory, even if you cannot imagine how that can happen. Faith means turning from everything else you have trusted in and putting your trust in God.

God allows certain things in our lives to strengthen and mature us. He sees the good He can bring out of any difficult situation. He has a place of peace for us in the midst of any trial if we put our faith in Him and seek Him.

Our difficult times perfect us, and that's why we can never lose faith in God to do something great, no matter what is happening.

The first thing God did in Gideon's army was to eliminate those who were fearful and full of doubt (Judges 7:3–8). It was better to have three hundred men who had faith and were not afraid, and who knew how to be ready for battle, than it was to have thirty-two thousand men who did not have faith and were not alert. God uses people with strong and fearless faith to bring glory to Him.

Sometimes we feel weak in the battle against the challenges of life because we become afraid and overwhelmed. But if we will have faith in the power of God as our defender, and stand ready for battle, He will bring us to victory in a way that we will be certain it was not because of our own strength and power.

We must have faith when we pray. Not faith in our faith or faith in our prayers, but faith in the One we are praying to. And we leave the final answer in His hands.

When Jesus and His disciples were in a boat and crossing over to the other side of the sea, a great storm came up and water began filling the boat (Mark 4:35–37). Jesus was asleep in the boat, so the disciples woke Him and said, "Teacher, do You not care that we are perishing?" (Mark 4:38). They assumed they were going to die. But Jesus arose and rebuked the wind, "and the wind ceased and there was a great calm" (Mark 4:39).

Then Jesus said to them, "Why are you so fearful? *How is it that you have no faith?*" (Mark 4:40, emphasis added). They had been with Him and had seen Him do many miracles, and *they still didn't have faith beyond what they could imagine.* That is too often our problem as well. Because we cannot imagine how God can ever get us out of the mess we are in, we think He won't come through for us. But with Jesus, you can always cross over to the other side of your problems. When a storm comes, remember that He is in the boat with you. You may think He doesn't care, because you are in the storm in the first place, but He can speak to the storms in your life and silence them.

In another terrible storm on the sea when the disciples were afraid in the boat, Jesus came walking toward them on the water. That frightened them even more because they thought He must be a ghost. Often when we are in the midst of a storm, we don't think there could possibly be a miraculous rescue by the Lord. We don't believe He can make us rise above it. Peter had enough faith to come walking out on the water to meet Him, but when he noticed the wind and started to sink, Jesus caught him, saying, *"You of little faith, why did you doubt?"* (Matthew 14:31, emphasis added). I am sure He must be speaking that same thing to us in the storms of our life when we start to lose faith.

Jesus said to His disciples, "Have faith in God . . . Whoever says to this mountain, 'Be removed and be cast into the sea,' and does not doubt in his heart, but believes that those things he says will be done, he will have whatever he says. Therefore I say to you, *whatever things you ask when you pray, believe that you receive them, and you will have them*" (Mark 11:22–24, emphasis added). Have faith. Don't doubt. Speak truth to the problem. Believe that you will receive the answer from God.

Jesus connects fear with lack of faith, and that's what tormenting fear is. "Without faith it is impossible to please Him, for he who comes to God must believe that He is, and that He is a rewarder of those who diligently seek Him" (Hebrews 11:6). You need *that* kind of faith now. Ask the Holy Spirit to grow it in you.

PRAYER POWER

Lord, I know that without faith it is impossible to please You (Hebrews 11:6). I don't want to go through life not pleasing You because I have little faith. I want to come to You believing that You are greater than anything I face, and that You reward those who seek You with all their heart. Give me the mountain-moving faith You speak of in Your Word (Mark 11:22–24). I confess the times I have doubted that You will always take care of me. Forgive me when I wonder if You will come through for me again. I confess my doubt as sin and ask Your forgiveness.

Help me to fully take up the shield of faith, without which I can never be protected from the enemy's plans against me. Teach me always to pray in faith without any doubting. I don't want to be double-minded and unstable because I doubt You (James 1:6–8). I don't want to be driven and tossed by the wind. Let it be to me according to my faith (Matthew 9:29). I know we "walk by faith, not by sight" (2 Corinthians 5:7). Help me not to see the things that make me afraid, but rather to see You in all Your power and glory, reaching to lift me above the storm and keep me from sinking.

In Jesus' name I pray.

WORD POWER

Count it all joy when you fall into various trials, knowing that the testing of your faith produces patience. But let patience have its perfect work, that you may be perfect and complete, lacking nothing.

JAMES 1:2–4

You have been grieved by various trials, that the genuineness of your faith, being

353

much more precious than gold that perishes, though it is tested by fire, may be found to praise, honor, and glory at the revelation of Jesus Christ.

1 PETER 1:6–7

Led to Follow God to the Company of Godly People

The Holy Spirit will always lead you to form your deepest relationships with godly people. These are the believers with whom you bond and spend time. That is not at all to say you are never to be with unbelievers, but the people who have *spiritual and personal input into your life* must be believers. The Holy Spirit will lead you away from spending time with people who do not produce the righteousness of God in your life.

Much is said in the Bible about the importance of godly friends, and we cannot ignore that. "Do not be deceived: 'Evil company corrupts good habits' " (1 Corinthians 15:33). Bad friends corrupt us. There is no doubt about it. That's why the Holy Spirit will always lead us to be with godly people.

One of the worst examples of the terrible influence of bad friends is David's son Amnon. He had a friend named Jonadab who "was a very crafty man" (2 Samuel 13:3). Amnon was infatuated with his half sister Tamar, and Jonadab, being the bad friend that he was, came up with a plan to trick Tamar into coming to Amnon's house. Amnon pretended to be sick and asked his father, King David, to send Tamar to take care of him. When she came to his sick bed, he raped her. Because he had no love or respect for her, once he got what he wanted, he hated her (2 Samuel 13:14–15).

King David was very angry when he found out that his son Amnon had raped Tamar. But David did nothing about it. This crime of incest was punishable by death, but David did absolutely nothing to follow God's command about this, nor did he even reprimand Amnon. The result was that later Absalom, Tamar's full brother, killed Amnon for this horrible crime against his sister. One corrupt friend influenced Amnon, and it destroyed the entire family.

When you are submitted to the Holy Spirit's leading in your life, He will lead you away from corrupting friends.

The Danites had never received their inheritance of land because they were not able to overpower their enemies. That's because they did not obey God and do what He wanted them to do. The Danites wanted more land, so they found another people who were quiet and peaceful and who had no leaders to oppose this takeover. These people were far from anyone who could protect them and *"they had no ties with anyone"* (Judges 18:7, emphasis added). In other words, they were good people, but they were isolated.

There are two main points of this story. One is that the Danites did what they wanted and attached God's name to it instead of really seeking the Lord's direction and following the leading of the Spirit of God. The other is that the quiet people were helpless because they had no connection or support from others.

We must be connected to other believers so we can stand strong with one another. We must be able to come to the defense of those who are under enemy attack. We cannot live entirely for ourselves — not in our family, not in our community — and we especially cannot live well without a church. I have seen it happen too often that even the most godly people get off in their thinking when they isolate themselves from other believers. Having no connection to a church body of believers allows us to become too self-focused, even though we try not to be and don't think we are.

Without godly people in your life who are sold out to the Lord, you will end up doing what you want. You will become guided by your own desires, opinions, and thoughts rather than by the Holy Spirit's leading.

PRAYER POWER

Lord, I pray You will lead me into the company of godly people and away from those who are not. Keep me from being influenced or corrupted by the people I allow to speak into my life. I see in Your Word the importance of being around strong believers so that we can sharpen one another (Proverbs 27:17). I know I can never fulfill my destiny apart from the people You put in my life who walk closely with You. Help us to strengthen and encourage one another and keep each other accountable. I know that "the righteous should choose his friends carefully, for the way of the wicked leads them astray" (Proverbs 12:26). Give me the discernment I need to know when a relationship does not glorify You. Help me to walk with wise people so that I will never do anything foolish (Proverbs 13:20).

For the relationships I have, or *will*

have, with people who do not know You, I pray I will be an important influence in their lives and draw them to You. I pray they will not stay unbelieving for long, but they will see Jesus in me, sense Your Holy Spirit working in my life, and want to know You. Send godly mentors and role models into my life who love You and exemplify Your faithfulness. Keep me from ever walking "in the counsel of the ungodly" (Psalm 1:1).

In Jesus' name I pray.

WORD POWER

If we walk in the light as He is in the light, we have fellowship with one another, and the blood of Jesus Christ His Son cleanses us from all sin.

1 JOHN 1:7

I am a companion of all who fear You, and of those who keep Your precepts.

PSALM 119:63

Led to Follow God to Care for Your Body

The Holy Spirit will always convict you of any sin you commit against your own body. Part of your service to God is to take care of yourself. Your body is the temple of His

Spirit, and you must not defile it in any way. Jesus paid a price for you, and you belong to Him.

"Do you not know that *your body is the temple of the Holy Spirit who is in you,* whom you have from God, and you are not your own? For you were bought at a price; therefore glorify God in your body and in your spirit, which are God's" (1 Corinthians 6:19–20, emphasis added). You must always value your body as the place where the Holy Spirit dwells.

The Holy Spirit will never lead you to do anything to harm your body in any way. If you are doing something that harms your body, you are not being led by the Spirit. You are instead being either led by your fleshly desires or the enemy of your body, soul, and mind. Because you have the Spirit in you, whenever you knowingly do something that hurts your body, you will feel a sense of remorse.

Don't expect your body to be perfect. Be grateful for what your body *can do* and refuse to criticize it for what you think it *should do.*

Ask the Holy Spirit to help you break destructive habits and pick up beneficial ones. I know how hard it is to break bad habits, but the Holy Spirit will help you every hour of every day. Tell God what you are struggling with in regard to caring for your body, and ask Him to lead you away from temptation and give you strength to do the right thing.

There is far too much in the Bible about observing a day of rest to ignore it — not to mention it is one of the Ten Commandments. Jesus observed the Sabbath and said it was established for our benefit. God did the work of creation for six days and then rested on the seventh, establishing the pattern we are to follow (Exodus 20:11). He is very clear about that. If God needed to take a day of rest, how much more do we need to do the same?

God wants us to be set apart for His purposes. We are to be different from the world in the way we act, think, and live. He wants us to observe the Sabbath as a holy day set apart for Him. In order to enter God's rest, we must cease from our work just as God did from His. "Let us therefore be diligent to enter that rest, lest anyone fall according to the same example of disobedience" (Hebrews 4:11). We honor God by observing the Sabbath one day a week.

The Holy Spirit is always moving you forward. Taking a Sabbath day is part of moving your life forward. In fact, you can stop the flow of blessing in your life by not obeying this commandment.

Ask the Holy Spirit to lead you in how you conduct your Sabbath day in order to keep it holy. Don't schedule anything that has to do with work on your day of rest. The times I have violated that, I have paid a heavy price. One time I had a writing deadline for which I was very late, and I worked on Sunday to write. While I got a lot done — and even though I was writing a book for and about the Lord — I paid a price in my body and mind. I got sick, hurt my back by being hunched over for hours writing, and I lost the peace and clarity I'd had. My mind needed rest too. And I was forced to take time to recover. It wasn't worth it. I have learned my lesson. It is not a price I am willing to pay anymore. God set up the law for *our* benefit and when we ignore it, we do so at our own peril. Trust me on this. Or better yet, trust God's Word.

PRAYER POWER
Lord, I pray You will give me the ability to walk away from any destructive habits I have with regard to caring for my body. Keep me ever mindful that my

body is Your temple and I need to take care of it. Help me to follow Your leading in every decision I make each day, especially what I put into my body and how I exercise. Help me to value my body enough to look after it. I confess the times I have been critical of my body and not grateful to You for it. Forgive me for that. Keep me from ever judging or mistreating it in any way.

Lord, help me to always observe a day of rest each week. Enable me to do it to Your glory so that I am rejuvenated in my body, mind, and emotions. Help me to give my body and mind rest from all else but Your voice to my heart. You know what is best for me because You created me. So I ask You to reveal to me all I need to do and avoid doing. Give me the discipline and self-control I need to carry it out. I know that self-control is a fruit of the Spirit, so I pray I will have such a manifestation of self-control that it will be explained no other way than as a gift from You.

In Jesus' name I pray.

Do you not know that you are the temple of God and that the Spirit of God dwells in you? If anyone defiles the temple of God, God will destroy him. For the temple of God is holy, which temple you are.

1 CORINTHIANS 3:16–17

I urge you, brothers and sisters, in view of God's mercy, to offer your bodies as a living sacrifice, holy and pleasing to God — this is your true and proper worship.

ROMANS 12:1 NIV

Led to Follow God to Resist the Enemy's Attacks

The enemy will always try to kill us, steal from us, and destroy us. That's why we must follow the leading of the Holy Spirit in order to know how to resist him. The Holy Spirit gave Jesus the conviction and knowledge that He must go in the wilderness to fast and pray and resist the enemy with God's Word.

When David found out that the Amalekites had come to the camp where he and his men and their families had been living and had plundered everything — including their wives and children — David asked God if he should pursue and overtake his enemies. His own men blamed David for what happened and wanted to kill him (1 Samuel 30:6). But David sought the Lord and found strength in Him.

We, too, must find our strength and peace in God when the enemy attacks — even when all seems to be against us and things are going terribly wrong. David heard from God that if they pursued their enemies, they would be victorious and recover all that had been lost to them (1 Samuel 30:8). There is no way David could have known that without revelation from God.

David had victory over his enemies because he did not *assume* that he was victorious or that he knew what to do. When we want the Lord to be with us and go out before us into the battle that the enemy wages against us, we must seek Him for direction.

When you persist in prayer against all that opposes you, you too can say as David did, "I have pursued my enemies and destroyed them; neither did I turn back again till they were destroyed" (2 Samuel 22:38).

The Holy Spirit in you is more powerful

than any enemy you will ever face. When you are under attack, remember that the enemy is already defeated and, in the end, you win (Revelation 12:10). *The Holy Spirit helps us to discern the lies of the enemy.* "Submit to God. Resist the devil and he will flee from you" (James 4:7).

One of the greatest stories in the Bible about spiritual warfare from God's perspective was when the king of Syria went to war with Israel. He was troubled because the prophet Elisha was telling the king of Israel what the Syrians were planning to do. So the king of Syria sent spies to find out where Elisha was, apparently not realizing the obvious — that the Holy Spirit would reveal to Elisha what the Syrian king was doing.

The Syrian army surrounded the city with horses and chariots, and when Elisha got up in the morning, he saw them gathered there. His fearful servant asked, "What shall we do?" Elisha answered, "Do not fear, *for those who are with us are more than those who are with them*" (2 Kings 6:16, emphasis added).

Elisha prayed, and said, "LORD, I pray, open his eyes that he may see." When the Lord opened the eyes of the servant, he saw that "*the mountain was full of horses and chariots of fire all around* Elisha" (2 Kings 6:17, emphasis added).

The same way Elisha prayed for his servant to see the invisible, we can pray to receive insight into our situation. When you are being attacked by the enemy, pray for your eyes to be opened so you can see things from God's perspective. Remember who is on your side. "If God is for us, who can be against us?" (Romans 8:31).

When the Syrians attacked, Elisha prayed, "Strike this people, I pray, with blindness." And God struck them with blindness exactly as Elisha prayed and led them into the hands of the Israelites (2 Kings 6:18).

Because of Jesus, the ruler of this world is judged, and we dominate the power of hell by overthrowing it in our lives with the truth of God's Word (John 16:11).

To believe means to be firmly established in the Lord. When the enemy encroaches upon your life — in your marriage; your children; your work; your ministry; your mind, soul, or body — humble yourself before God and declare your dependence upon Him. Have complete faith in His Word and pray for His intervention. Fast and pray to God's glory and for the leading of His Spirit. Worship Him in the beauty of His holiness. This is a powerful combination that firmly establishes you in the Lord, and no forces of hell can prevail against you when you resist the enemy's attack in this way. Even when there appears to be no way out of the threat, God will do something to bring about victory you never dreamed possible.

Praise and worship is one of the most powerful weapons of warfare. The Spirit of God will infuse you with His power, strength, peace, and joy as you worship Him.

The Holy Spirit will always lead you to resist the enemy. When you hear the lies of the enemy, worship God. When the Israelites worshipped Him, the enemy became confused, fought against one another, and completely destroyed themselves. Our praise confuses the enemy and he hates it.

Remember, you don't fight alone. "The LORD will fight for you" (Exodus 14:14) and you can have peace in the midst of the battle. Don't be afraid to pray for a miracle. Be afraid of what will happen if you *don't*.

PRAYER POWER

Lord, I pray You will help me to stand against all that the enemy wants to do in my life. Help me to recognize when he is attacking me so that I will refuse to endure his tactics. Thank You for delivering me from the evil one, and that You will continue to do so in the future as well (Matthew 6:13). Help me to put on "the whole armor of God" so that I can powerfully withstand whatever the enemy attempts to do (Ephesians 6:11). Thank You, Lord, that You will guard me from the evil one (2 Thessalonians 3:3) because one of the reasons You came was to "destroy the works of the devil" (1 John 3:8).

I know that even though I walk in the flesh, I do not war according to the flesh. "For the weapons of our warfare are not carnal but mighty in God for pulling down strongholds" (2 Corinthians 10:4). Thank You that You have delivered me from the hands of the enemy, and You are greater and stronger than his most powerful weapon. Thank You that "the angel of the LORD encamps all around those who fear Him, and delivers them" (Psalm 34:7). Thank You that You "will deliver me from every evil work" (2 Timothy 4:18). Thank You that the enemy is under Your feet (Ephesians 1:22). Whenever the enemy tries to erect a stronghold in my life, I pray You will strike it down.

In Jesus' name I pray.

By this I know that You are well pleased with me, because my enemy does not triumph over me.

PSALM 41:11

So shall they fear the name of the LORD from the west, and His glory from the rising of the sun; when the enemy comes in like a flood, the Spirit of the LORD will lift up a standard against him.

ISAIAH 59:19

Led to Follow God to the Right Place at the Right Time

The Holy Spirit will always lead us to the right place at the right time. And we must follow His leading, because the truth is that we cannot get there on our own.

In the beginning of his life and reign as king, David sought the leading of the Lord before he did anything because he wanted to be exactly where God wanted him to be. It is said that David became great *because God was with him* (2 Samuel 5:10). God was with *him* because *he* was with *God.*

David had success after success and conquest after conquest, but then he grew lazy and overconfident in himself. Things began to change when David stopped asking for the leading of the Spirit of God before he took action. So it was in the spring, "at the time when kings go out to battle," that David didn't go with his men as he should have but instead remained comfortable in Jerusalem (2 Samuel 11:1).

David wasn't where he was supposed to be, and he wasn't doing what he was supposed to be doing.

David was up on his roof watching the woman next door take a bath. His lust for this married woman — Bathsheba — became stronger than his love for God. His will to have her was greater than his desire for *God's* will. Her husband, Uriah, was out on the battlefield when David seduced her. When Bathsheba became pregnant, David called her husband back from the battlefield so he could spend time with his wife. That way David and Bathsheba's love affair and subsequent love child could be covered up.

What David didn't plan on was that Uriah was an honorable man who felt he could not go to the comfort of his own house and wife while his men were suffering on the battlefield. (Something David should have felt but didn't.) When David saw he could not get Uriah to cover his sin for him, David instructed that Uriah be put in a vulnerable position on the battlefield so he would be killed. When Uriah died, David took Bathsheba as his wife.

In just a brief time of not following the leading of the Lord but rather following the lust of his own flesh, David committed adultery, sired an illegitimate child, and then committed murder to cover it up. He stopped seeking the will of God and became greedy, lustful, selfish, callous, evil, and murderous. He succumbed to the will of David. If he had sought the Lord about what he was to do, where he was to be, and when he was to go there, none of this would have happened.

God sent the prophet Nathan to David to confront him on what he had done. God said that now "the sword shall never depart from your house, because you have despised Me" (2 Samuel 12:10). David confessed that he had sinned against the Lord. As punishment, David would not die, but his child with Bathsheba would (2 Samuel 12:14). The result of sin and an unholy union is death in one form or another. David fasted and pleaded with God for the child, but the child died anyway (2 Samuel 12:15–18).

The consequences when we do not allow the Holy Spirit to lead us to the right place at the right time are not worth the selfish plea-sure of taking things into our own hands and disobeying God.

Whenever you are not where God wants you to be, you are in danger. That's why you must ask the Holy Spirit each day to lead you to the right place at the right time. Even when you have a sense of God's leading, keep praying and testing it against God's Word. Be convinced that the only things we accomplish that are good and lasting are those that are done with the leading of the Holy Spirit.

God puts us in certain places at certain times in order to serve His purposes. Finding the narrow path to life means following the leading of the Holy Spirit.

Jesus said that "narrow is the gate and difficult is the way which leads to life, and there are few who find it" (Matthew 7:14). The gate to life is found by walking a narrow path. You can only find it by walking according to the Word of God and following the leading of the Holy Spirit. It is found by being dependent upon God for every step you take. The path to life is not all over the place. It is found by moving forward step by step with God.

When you live in obedience to God, do

what His Word says to do, and follow His Holy Spirit, you will end up where you are supposed to be. But you must decide to go only where the Spirit of God leads you. Moses said to God, "If Your Presence does not go with us, do not bring us up from here" (Exodus 33:15). Determine to do nothing outside of the leading of the Holy Spirit and the presence of God.

You never know where the Spirit of the Lord will lead you. He will take you to places you never dreamed He would.

Christopher Columbus discovered America in 1492. In the only book he ever wrote — *Book of Prophesies* — he said he could not have reached America *without prayer and the guidance of the Holy Spirit.* He said, "There is no question that the inspiration was from the Holy Spirit."* We, too, must be able to say that the inspiration for all we do is from the Holy Spirit and we will follow Him anywhere.

Be submitted to the Lord and open to hearing His Spirit speak to your heart. *Be willing*

* Mark A. Beliles and Stephen K. McDowell, *America's Providential History* (Charlottesville, PA: Providence Press, 1989), 45.

to follow the leading of His Spirit when He gives you direction. *Read* His Word. *Worship* Him and pray. The more you do all this, the more you will hear Him speaking to your heart, and the more you will be led by His Spirit. He will give you a deep sense of peace and understanding of the way you should go.

PRAYER POWER

Lead me, Holy Spirit, into everything You have for me today. Help me to hear Your voice guiding me in all things. I submit myself to You — my words, thoughts, and actions — and pray I can accomplish Your will. Speak to me and help me to hear Your voice speaking to my heart. Guide me with Your Holy Spirit to the place I should be. Help me to not resist Your direction or, worse yet, to miss hearing You entirely.

Lord, help me to do what's right in all things. When there are times that it is hard to determine what the right thing is, reveal it to me by Your Spirit. If ever I want to go *my* own way and it isn't the right way, open my eyes to the truth. Enable me to be so submitted to You that I will hear Your voice leading me to do the right thing in every situation. Help me to do what is right and good in Your sight, Lord, so that it may be well with me, and that I can go in and possess all that You have for me (Deuteronomy 6:18). I want to always be in the right place at the right time, and I know that is not possible unless I follow the leading of Your Spirit and I wait for Your direction.

In Jesus' name I pray.

WORD POWER

Your ears shall hear a word behind you, saying, "This is the way, walk in it," whenever you turn to the right hand or whenever you turn to the left.

ISAIAH 30:21

Wait on the LORD; be of good courage, and He shall strengthen your heart; wait, I say, on the LORD!

PSALM 27:14

12
LED TO LEAD

To have God's Holy Spirit in us is the greatest gift imaginable. To be used by God for His purposes because of that is astounding. There is a direct correlation between how much we give place to the Holy Spirit in our lives and how much He can use us. If we don't acknowledge Him at all, the realization of God's purpose for us is hindered. If we embrace Him wholeheartedly and invite Him to work in us, He accomplishes His will through us.

Don't be afraid of what the Holy Spirit might do in and through you. Be afraid of what your life will be like if God's will is not done.

The Holy Spirit will always lead you toward wholeness and spiritual maturity. The main reason God does that is not only for *your* greatest good, but also for the blessing of others. God wants to use you to help others and to point them to Christ.

The problem is that too often we draw

back because we think we are inadequate to the task. I can hear it now. "But I can't speak well." "I'm shy." "I don't want to offend anyone." "I'm not comfortable talking to people about spiritual things." "I'm not good enough." "I'm too busy." "I am not perfect." "I don't always do the right thing." "I don't know enough." "I don't have the right clothes." "My house needs cleaning." "My bangs are too short." "I have a blemish." "I've made some bad decisions." "My business is struggling." (Did I leave anything out?) I know this because these were all my excuses at one time.

Please! Let me release you from all fear! God wants you to lead people to the truth about who He is and the hope they have in Jesus because of what He has done for them, but that doesn't mean you will have to stand before a crowd with a microphone. He will not put you in front of a stadium of people to proclaim the gospel. Well, maybe He will . . . but only if you are called to that. God is going to equip you for what He has for *you* to do.

If you are learning to hear God's voice in His Word and to follow His Holy Spirit in your life, *He can use you.* If you worship Him in spirit and in truth and are willing to be separate from sin, the world, temptation, your past, and anything else that tries to draw you away from God, *He can use you.* If you are being transformed in your mind, emotions, and character, and are being led to see purpose for your life, *He can use you.* If the reason you get up every day is to serve God with the gifts He has put in you and His call on your life, *He can use you.* If He is leading you to produce good fruit, and to discern when He is guiding, blessing, and protecting you, *He can use you.* If you are praying for loved ones, strangers, and people God brings to your mind, *He can use you.* If you are being led to follow God to an intimate day-by-day walk with Him, to purify the words you speak, to have greater faith, to be in the company of godly people, to resist enemy attack, and to end up at the right place at the right time, *He can use you.* If you are humble and have a teachable and repentant heart, He can use you.

You don't have to be a Bible scholar, a preacher, or someone perfect. You just have to be yourself and simply give a reason for the hope that is in you. You already have the love of God in your heart because you have the Spirit of God in you, and you can extend it to others as God directs you. When you speak the words God gives you, His Holy Spirit will add His power to them.

Paul said, "My speech and my preaching were not with persuasive words of human wisdom, but in *demonstration of the Spirit and of power*" (1 Corinthians 2:4, emphasis added). It wasn't his words that brought people to the Lord; it was the Holy Spirit manifesting Himself through him that did it. And Paul deliberately didn't make it about him, so that people's faith would *"not be in the wisdom of men but in the power of God"* (1 Corinthians 2:5, emphasis added).

The Bible says that "the kingdom of God is not in word but in power" (1 Corinthians 4:20). It won't be your power or your words that will bring life to people; it will be *the power of the Holy Spirit anointing the words God leads you to say.* So the pressure is not on you to deliver. All you have to do is come humbly before the Lord and invite the Holy Spirit to work through you to touch the lives of others.

Jesus was conceived by the miraculous power of the Holy Spirit, and He was sinless His entire life, yet He did not move into any kind of ministry without being empowered by the Holy Spirit of God, which happened when He was baptized and the Holy Spirit came upon Him. From then on He was led by the Spirit to declare that God's kingdom was at hand and to demonstrate that in miraculous ways. If Jesus needed to be empowered by the Holy Spirit before He moved out in ministry, how much more should *we* follow *His* example and not move in ministry without His power?

I know a family who moved to a foreign country 50 years ago on the mission field and were nearly destroyed. Their marriage broke up, their children walked away from God, and they came home broken and defeated. The wife says to this day that it was because they did not have that extra outpouring of Holy Spirit power. They were with a church that never taught about the Holy Spirit, and so they didn't have a chance against the forces of hell in the place where they were.

God wants you to "let your light so shine before men, that they may see your good works and glorify your Father in heaven" (Matthew 5:16). Your light shines when you receive Jesus and the Holy Spirit manifests Himself in and through you to others, and you humbly give God glory. Letting His light shine through you is a big part of your ministry.

Ministry is what we do in the love of God to help other people, and to bring them into a relationship with Him through Jesus Christ.

■ ■ ■ ■

Having the Holy Spirit in us allows the power of God to flow through us to a world in desperate need of the Lord. And time is growing shorter. And more serious. The stakes are high. People are hungry for the supernatural. They want something real. We cannot inhibit the Holy Spirit's work if we want to affect the world positively. We need Him to move in power in us more than ever before. We cannot stand strong in the Lord, nor can we help *others* stand strong, if we don't allow the Spirit of God to be strong in us.

God wants us to pray that laborers are sent into the harvest of souls. Jesus said to His disciples that "the harvest truly is plentiful, but the laborers are few" (Matthew 9:37). You are one of God's laborers who will draw people to Jesus. This does not mean you have to go to the jungles of Africa. It means you need to pray that God will open up opportunities to touch others wherever you are. It may be just next door or wherever you happen to be in the course of a day.

Perhaps at some point you have been approached by someone trying insensitively to push Jesus on you, and you ran screaming internally from the encounter, and you remember how uncomfortable that was and how much you hated it and you don't ever want to do that to anyone. I understand. I have experienced that too, and I didn't like it either. I don't want you to ever do anything like that to someone. But you never will. That was done *without* the Holy Spirit. The Holy Spirit doesn't force. He draws. He doesn't pounce, annoy, impose, or trap. He *leads.* The Holy Spirit is not loveless. He is tender and loving. A person led by the Spirit will be that way too.

Jesus said, "Whoever desires to save his life will lose it, but whoever loses his life for My sake and the gospel's will save it . . . For whoever is ashamed of Me and My words in this adulterous and sinful generation, of him the Son of Man also will be ashamed when He comes in the glory of His Father with the holy angels" (Mark 8:35,38). It is a privilege to lose our life for Him, and we do that when we make living our life for *Him* a priority over living life for *ourselves.* We never want Him to be ashamed of us because we are embarrassed to share Jesus with other people. But we must always be sensitive to the Holy Spirit's leading.

Led to Lead Others to Find Hope in the Lord

You are valuable in your realm of influence, and you can be used by God in the lives of certain people in a way no one else can. Even if you *feel* you have nothing to offer, this is not true. You have the Holy Spirit in you. You can help people lift their eyes to the Lord, where their hope comes from.

When you find your hope in the Lord, you cannot just keep it to yourself. You have to share it with others.

Hope means you anticipate that something good is going to happen to you, because you are God's child and He loves you and takes care of you. Do you realize how many people never feel that? They need you to tell them about the hope you have and how they can have that same hope too. They need to understand why they can put their hope in God.

Because you are guided by the Holy Spirit, you will be able to *comfort, guide,* and *teach* others. If you have a heart for people who are hurting or feel hopeless and discouraged in their situation, ask the Holy Spirit to help you minister love, hope, and encouragement to those whom God brings into your life. He will give you the right words at the right time. He will open up opportunities to talk with a friend or acquaintance, or you may be sitting on a plane or bus with a stranger who may be intrigued by the hope they sense in you, and a door will open. Remember, people don't want to be impressed with your abilities; they want to hear how God can help *them* get rid of their emptiness and pain.

When the opportunity arises to minister the love and hope of God to someone, the Holy Spirit will enable you to do it in a way that will make a lasting impact on that person's life. And it will glorify God in the most effective and powerful way. When God opens the door, don't worry about what to say. Just be God's love extended.

PRAYER POWER

Lord, help me to communicate the hope I have in You to others who need to hear about it. Teach me to sense when someone is discouraged and hopeless. Enable me to "always be ready to give a defense to everyone who asks" me about my reason for the hope within me (1 Peter 3:15). Enable me to lead others to see the hope *they* have in You, as well. I know Your eye is on those who fear You and who put their hope in You and Your mercy (Psalm 33:18). I commit to You as a laborer in Your field and say, "I will hope continually, and will praise You yet more and more" (Psalm 71:14).

I know happiness comes from serving You as Lord and putting my hope in You (Psalm 146:5). When I am speaking to someone about the hope I have, I pray that You, "the God of hope," will fill that person with a sense of hope like they have never known before (Romans 15:13). Help me to remember to tell the person I am speaking to that whenever he feels hopeless about anything, turning to You in prayer and reading Your Word can ignite hope within him. Enable me to convince him that putting his hope in You, the God of the impossible, means there will always be hope for anything in his life.

In Jesus' name I pray.

WORD POWER

O Israel, hope in the LORD; for with the LORD there is mercy, and with Him is abundant redemption.

PSALM 130:7

We through the Spirit eagerly wait for

the hope of righteousness by faith.

GALATIANS 5:5

Led to Lead Others to Know the Truth

It is only by the leading of the Spirit of truth in *us* that we can lead *others* to see the truth about Jesus. Our ministry to others is nothing without the Holy Spirit working through us. Only *He* can open people's hearts. Only He can give us words to say.

Part of leading others to the truth has to do with leading sinners away from sin. It doesn't mean we sit in judgment on anyone. It is not done in an arrogant, superior manner. Anything less than our humility before God will produce nothing. It is done in the love of God, with sincere concern for that person, and only by the leading of the Holy Spirit.

If you see someone who is living the wrong way and you know their life is about to go over a cliff because of the seeds of flesh they are sowing — or have sown in the past — ask the Holy Spirit to lead you as to what you should say to help them get on the right track. "If a man is overtaken in any trespass, you who are spiritual restore such a one in a spirit of gentleness, considering yourself lest you also be tempted" (Galatians 6:1). Those last five words mean you should not put yourself in situations where there is temptation for you.

Ask God to show you how He wants you to use the truth in His Word to respond to the needs of others. You may be a *shower of mercy* to those who are hurting, an *encourager* with words so others can find hope in the Lord, a faithful *speaker* of truth to someone who needs to hear about God, a *server* of hospitality to those who need to feel cared for, or a *leader* of others into a deeper walk with the Lord (Romans 12:4–8). Each one of these is a way to share the truth about Jesus.

You were "created in Christ Jesus for good works" (Ephesians 2:10). This is the reason you are here. The Holy Spirit will lead you in the use of your gifts to help others, and He will give you the spiritual gifts you need. God wants us to be "zealous for spiritual gifts," but let it only be "for the edification of the church that you seek to excel" (1 Corinthians 14:12).

Each of us is unique, and God will gift us uniquely to be used by Him. That's why we must never be jealous of another's ministry. God decides who does what. Just concern yourself with being led by the Holy Spirit in *your* ministry. You are there to serve God by serving others as the Spirit of God leads *you*. Lead them to the truth of God's Word. Speak the message God has given you. Try to be known as someone who lives in the ways of God, especially as a person of truth. That may impress people favorably more than anything else.

Today — like never before in our lifetime — we see the world shaking. Some things are shaking loose. Other things are being shaken down — some to complete destruction. We all sense that there is coming a spiritual temblor, the magnitude of which we have never seen or imagined. Those who face the future *without* the Spirit of God in their lives will not be able to navigate through what will happen. They will be sucked into it like a mighty tsunami and pulled wherever the force of it takes them. Without the Holy Spirit, they will not have the revelation they need to even comprehend what is going on in the world, let alone have the power and hope to rise above it. Lacking knowledge of the ultimate truth, they will live in confusion.

People must hear the truth so they can decide whether to accept or reject it. If we believers don't come out of our comfort zone to reach others, who will? That's why

God gives us His Holy Spirit, to be made whole and holy and prepared to lead others to the truth, so they can have eternal life and fulfill their purpose in Christ.

PRAYER POWER

Lord, I know how much *I* need You, and that makes me especially sensitive to how much other people need You as well. I don't ever want to be the one to stand in the way of someone coming to know You because I have hesitated to answer Your call to ministry. I pray I will be used powerfully to be a witness to the truth of Your Word and the truth of who You are. Lead me, Holy Spirit, whenever I am around someone who needs to know more about You. Even if I am in a situation where I don't have the opportunity to say anything about You at the time, I pray Your love will shine through me to them. Show me how I can communicate Your love in tangible ways so that they will remember and identify Your Spirit working through me.

Lord, I know I cannot lead others to the truth if I don't fully know the truth and live by it myself. Help me to not only understand Your Word but be able to demonstrate its power in my life. Enable me to communicate it clearly in a way that is life changing. Enable me to "be a minister of Jesus Christ to the Gentiles, ministering the gospel of God," and being led by Your Spirit (Romans 15:16). Help me to never be "lagging in diligence" but to always be "fervent in spirit" serving You in all I do (Romans 12:11).

In Jesus' name I pray.

WORD POWER

When He has come, He will convict the world of sin, and of righteousness, and of judgment.

JOHN 16:8

Do you despise the riches of His goodness, forbearance, and longsuffering, not knowing that the goodness of God leads you to repentance?

ROMANS 2:4

Led to Lead Others to Pray in Power

One of the most important things you can ever do for someone, besides leading them to the Lord, is teach them to pray. The most effective way to do that is to pray *for* them and then pray *with* them when they are open to it. By praying *with* them, I mean the two of you are praying aloud together.

Prayer is a great and powerful ministry that anyone can do anytime. It is amazing how many people are open to being prayed for when you simply say, "Can I pray for you?" I have had people with no spiritual commitment to God at all be open to being prayed for.

When someone shares a particular need, you have the perfect opportunity to pray for them. As someone's heart opens for you to share about the Lord, you can take advantage of that opportunity to pray *with* them. In prayer you can encourage them to seek God's direction for their lives so they will understand their purpose and how to fulfill it. You don't have to make anything happen. God will open doors. People will see Jesus in you — even though they don't yet know Him — and they will be attracted to you because of it. And they will sense that they can trust you when you pray for them.

Don't be afraid to pray for others because you are concerned that your prayers might not be answered. It's your job to pray and God's job is to answer. You just have to do your job and let God do His.

Paul instructed us to "bear one another's burdens, and so fulfill the law of Christ"

(Galatians 6:2). The greatest way to lighten a person's burden is not only to pray for them but to teach them how to pray as well. Jesus said "if two of you agree on earth concerning anything that they ask, it will be done for them by My Father in heaven. For where two or three are gathered together in My name, I am there in the midst of them" (Matthew 18:19–20). This is the ultimate case for praying with other people. Just two people praying together, and you are guaranteed to have the presence of Jesus with you. How can you not?

God will bring people into your life for whom you are to pray. But if you are walking down the street in New York City at rush hour on the Saturday before Christmas, don't think that everyone around you is there to benefit from your prayers. Yet there may be one who stands out to you in a restaurant or a store, whom you know God has brought into your life at that moment, and you may be the only glimpse of Jesus they will see for a while. Pray silently that their heart will be open to the Lord. Then simply show the love of God to them in some way.

Smile and let them go before you in line. Help them with something they are struggling to hold. Encourage them with a greeting. You have no idea how much some people need to be affirmed that someone sees them as a person of worth. If you don't get to say anything more than "God bless you" to her, she will sense the Holy Spirit of God in you even though she cannot identify that yet, and it will give her a sense of hope. Someday she may recognize that same Spirit in someone else and realize what she was sensing. Even if you only silently pray for that person without her knowledge, that prayer has enough power to draw her into a relationship with God in the future.

Don't become discouraged if you do not directly lead people to the Lord. God has many laborers in the field. Some plant seeds, some water, and others reap. The reapers are no more valuable than the planters or the waterers. The reapers would have nothing to reap without them.

Prayer is the means by which we help others get close to God. If your ministry never went beyond praying for or with other people and teaching them to pray, you will have changed lives for eternity.

PRAYER POWER
Lord, I ask You to teach me how to pray in power for other people so that

they can learn to pray in power as well. Enable me to lead others in prayer whenever the opportunity presents itself. Keep me from holding back out of fear or self-doubt. Help me to be serious and watchful in my prayers at all times so that I never miss Your leading (1 Peter 4:7). Holy Spirit of God, I pray You will give me the words to say when I don't know exactly how to pray. Help me to never be at a loss for words. Teach me to recognize *whom* I should pray with, *when* the time is right, and *what* I should pray.

I know Your eyes are always on the righteous and Your ears are open to our prayers (1 Peter 3:12). I am grateful You hear my prayers because I have put my trust in You (1 Chronicles 5:20). I pray You will help me to see who is suffering and needs prayer. Enable me to be an encouragement to people and never an annoyance. As we pray together about their troubles, help them see You are the only one who can save them "out of their distresses" (Psalm 107:19). Help me to lead others to pray. When I pray for them, answer in a powerful way that convinces them You are real.

In Jesus' name I pray.

Ask, and it will be given to you; seek, and you will find; knock, and it will be opened to you. For everyone who asks receives, and he who seeks finds, and to him who knocks it will be opened.

LUKE 11:9–10

Whatever things you ask in prayer, believing, you will receive.

MATTHEW 21:22

Led to Lead Others to Fulfill Their Purpose

God will use you to help others find His purpose for their lives. He will put people in your path, and you can pray for them to understand His will for their life. Most likely you will pray *with* them and seek God together for the answer. The Holy Spirit will equip you to disciple them in that way so you never have to rely only on your own abilities. "He who calls you is faithful, who also will do it" (1 Thessalonians 5:24).

When God calls you to disciple someone, He will prepare you and enable you to do that.

To disciple someone means to spend time with that person sharing all you know about the Lord so they can become strong in Him and fulfill God's purpose and call on their life.

The young women I have discipled give me great joy when I see what wonderful people they are and how powerfully they live their lives for the Lord. They are not perfect people who became more perfect. They had serious struggles God has helped them overcome. One of them has become so zealous for God that she goes where angels fear to tread in order to tell people about Jesus. Discipling someone can be very rewarding. Don't worry if you feel that your abilities in this regard are limited. I felt that way too, but you can be reassured that the Holy Spirit in you will enable you to do far more than you ever thought you could.

Having a ministry does not mean you have to pastor a church, host a TV show, go on the mission field, or write a bestselling book. It means you are led by the Lord to help someone in some way. Jesus said that the second greatest commandment is "You shall love your neighbor as yourself" (Matthew 22:39). This could be a family member, a coworker, a person on the street, someone in your neighborhood, church, or wherever. Helping a person in their walk with the Lord is a great calling.

We are Christ's body on the earth. We are

His hands extended. Jesus said when we do things for others, we are doing it for Him (Matthew 25:35–40). Isn't it amazing to think that to the degree we bless others we bless Jesus as well? When you help others find the Lord and then their God-given purpose in life, think how this must please Him. You have helped to bring another child of His into His kingdom for all eternity, and you have helped them to find the right path here and now. You do what you hear the Holy Spirit leading you to do, and God will anoint what you have done in order to bring life-changing results.

Jesus said to make disciples of all nations. That doesn't mean you have to go to every nation. It means you can touch anyone anywhere, anytime and pray that the ripple effect will eventually touch every nation. Jesus promised that He will be with you always (Matthew 28:20). So until His return, do what He leads you to do, beginning right where you are, and lead others to do the same.

PRAYER POWER

Lord, enable me to use the gifts You have put in me to help others. Teach me to clearly understand Your leading in my ministry to the people You bring into my life. I don't want to move in the flesh, but to always lay a foundation in prayer beforehand so that I will find the people whose hearts are open and ready to receive from You. I pray You will always give me the right words to say to communicate Your love for those whom You put in my path. Enable me to help them find the purpose for which they were created. If I am to disciple someone, show me clearly and enable me to do it.

Give me words of healing for anyone whose heart is broken. Help me to proclaim that You, Jesus, have come to bring "liberty to the captives, and the opening of the prison to those who are bound" (Isaiah 61:1). Enable me to communicate that You have come to comfort those who mourn and "give them beauty for ashes, the oil of joy for mourning, the garment of praise for the spirit of heaviness" so that You may be glorified (Isaiah 61:3). Teach me how to point people to the call You have on their life. May I never "grow weary while doing good, for in due season" I know I will reap if I "do not lose heart" (Galatians 6:9).

In Jesus' name I pray.

All authority has been given to Me in heaven and on earth. Go therefore and make disciples of all the nations, baptizing them in the name of the Father and of the Son and of the Holy Spirit, teaching them to observe all things that I have commanded you; and lo, I am with you always, even to the end of the age.

MATTHEW 28:18–20

Whatever you ask in My name, that I will do, that the Father may be glorified in the Son. If you ask anything in My name, I will do it.

JOHN 14:13–14